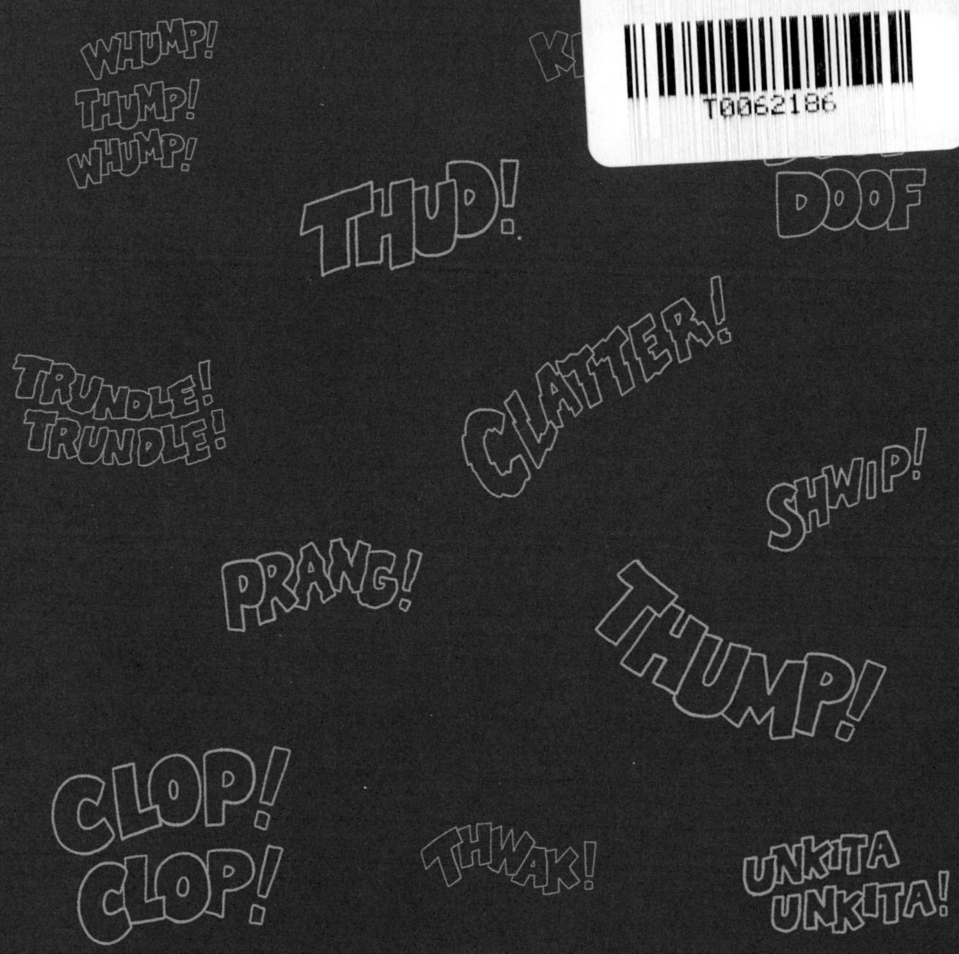
WHUMP!
THUMP!
WHUMP!
THUD!
DOOF
TRUNDLE!
TRUNDLE!
CLATTER!
SHWIP!
PRANG!
THUMP!
CLOP!
CLOP!
THWAK!
UNKITA
UNKITA!

BEEEP!
BEEEP!
BEEEP!

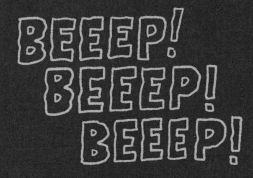

KEEP IT DOWN UP THERE!

KEEP IT DOWN UP THERE!

THE EVERYDAY SHENANIGANS OF NOISY NEIGHBORS

LUKE McGARRY

CHRONICLE BOOKS
SAN FRANCISCO

Library of Congress Cataloging-in-Publication Data available.

ISBN 978-1-7972-2441-1

Manufactured in China.

MIX
Paper | Supporting responsible forestry
FSC™ C008047
FSC
www.fsc.org

Design by Maggie Edelman.

10 9 8 7 6 5 4 3 2 1

Chronicle books and gifts are available at special quantity discounts to corporations, professional associations, literacy programs, and other organizations. For details and discount information, please contact our premiums department at corporatesales@chroniclebooks.com or at 1-800-759-0190.

Chronicle Books LLC
680 Second Street
San Francisco, California 94107
www.chroniclebooks.com

We've all been there—you're unwinding on the couch, scrolling through Zillow, and dreaming of the day you have a parking spot and a dishwasher, when suddenly you hear an abominable racket coming from the apartment above you. Unit 3E has jolted you from your reverie, as you cry out toward the ceiling in anguish, "Just how many smoothies can one person make in a day?"

Of course, this book is just a bit of fun—tongue firmly planted in cheek. If you or a loved one are a break-dancing, grape-treading, primal scream therapist, more power to you! But you should be aware, your noisy hobbies have made you the bane of your downstairs neighbor's existence.

Whether living under an Irish dancer, a budding drummer, or anyone else with a cacophonous craft, it is a truth self-evident: Sharing spaces can be difficult. Apartment neighbors—can't live with them, can't live without them (although we all dream about it . . . and in-unit laundry).

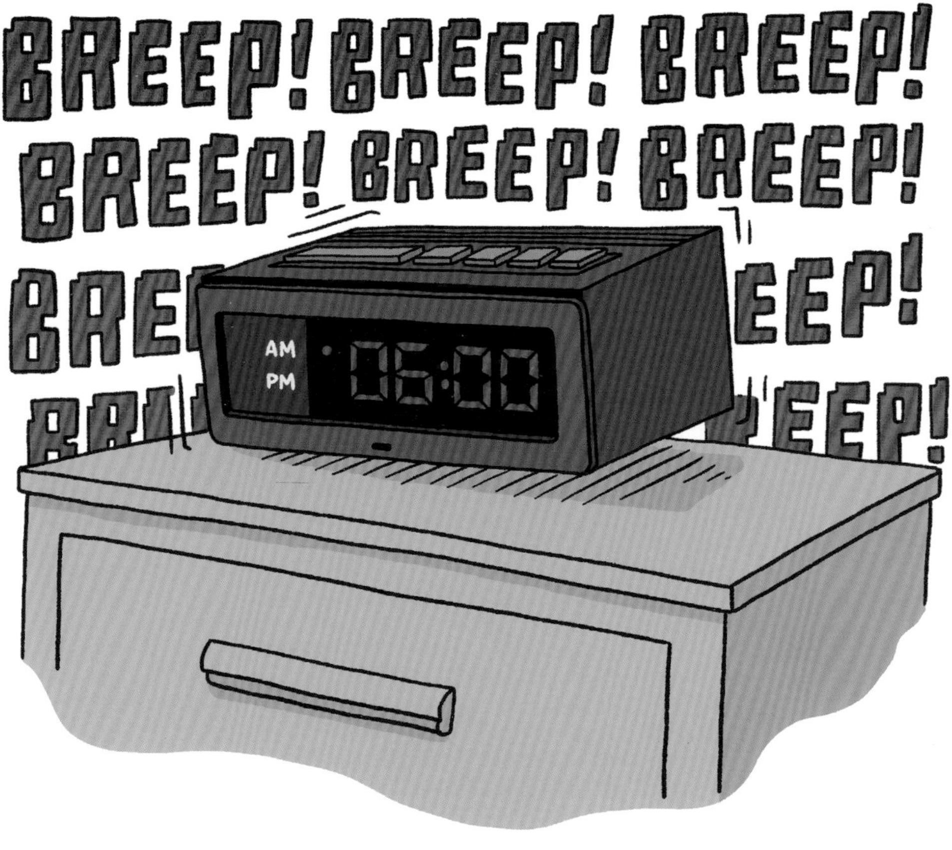
BREEP! BREEP! BREEP!
BREEP! BREEP! BREEP!
AM
PM
06:00

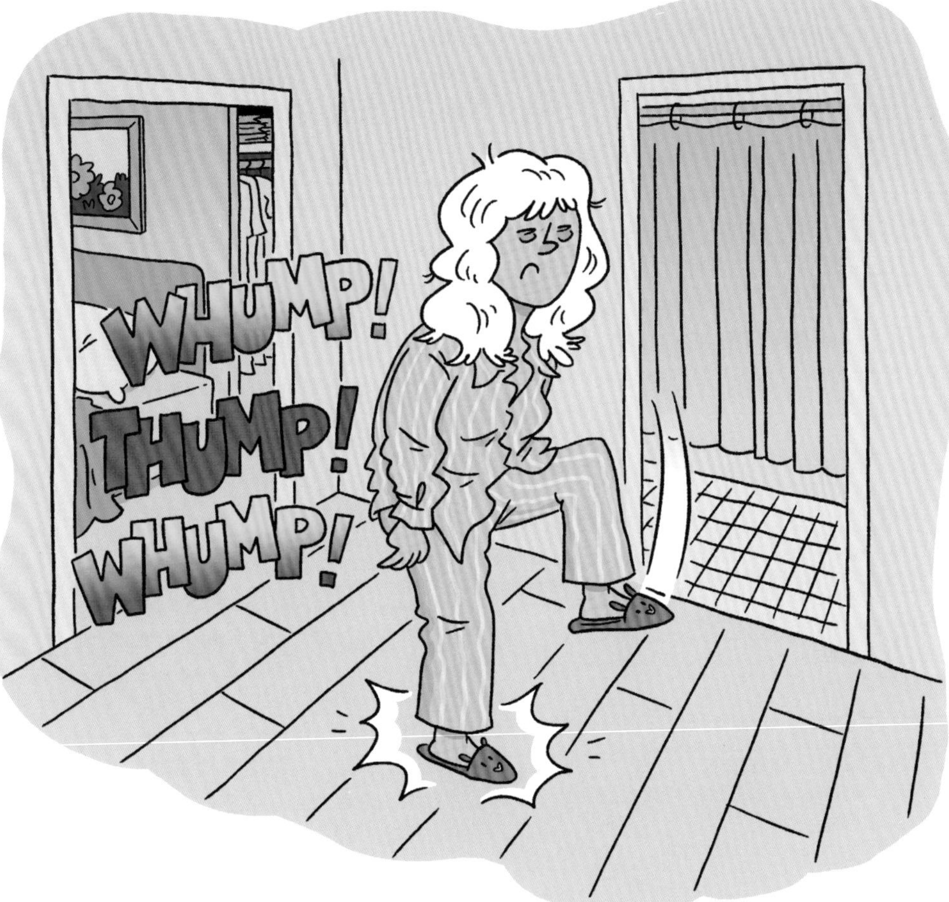
WHUMP!
THUMP!
WHUMP!

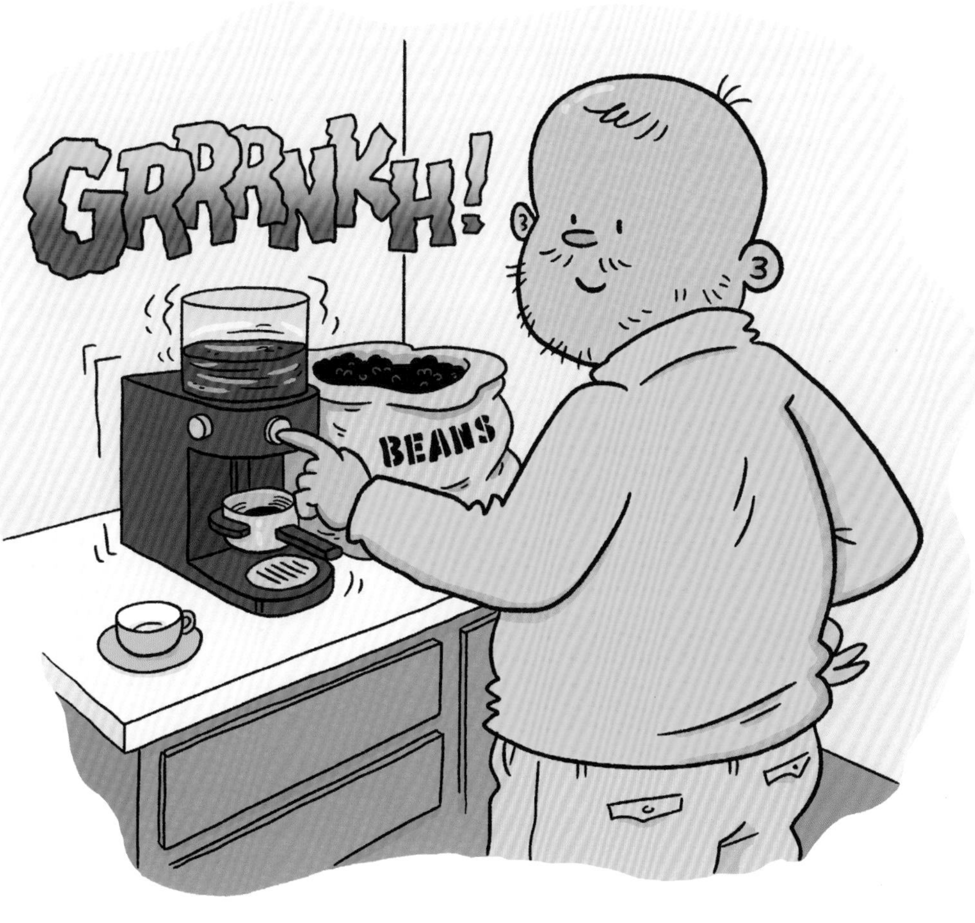
GRRRNKH!
BEANS

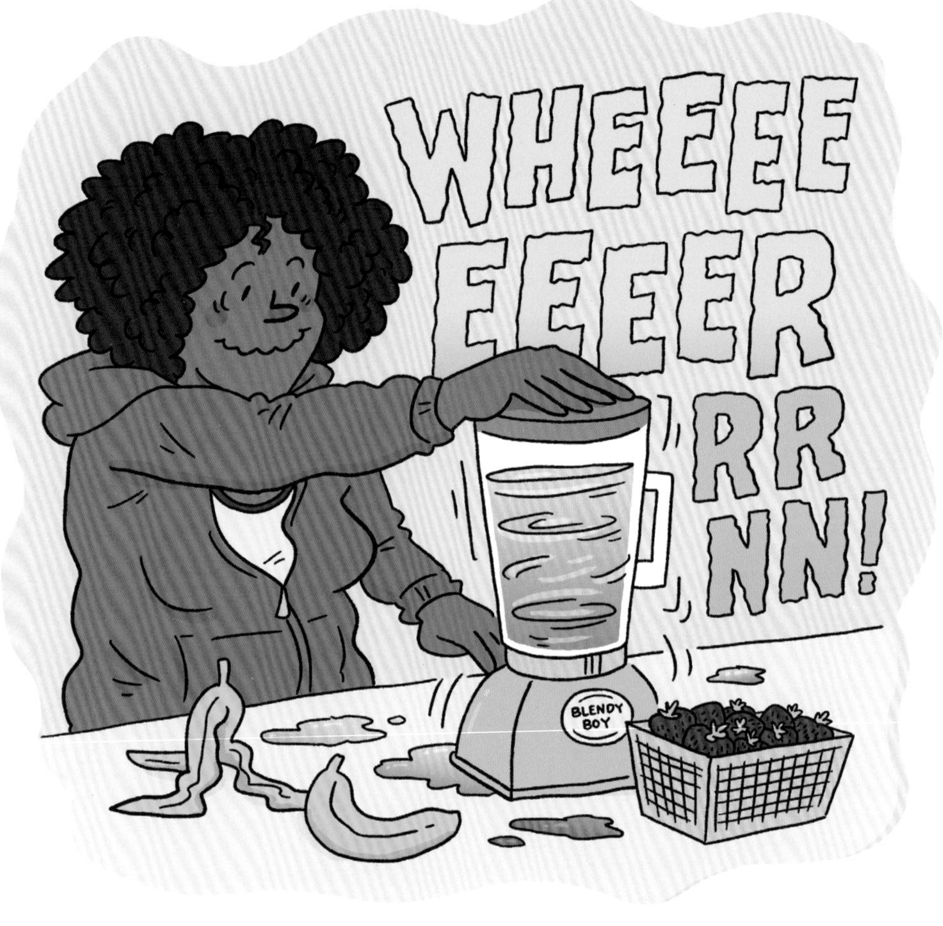
WHEEEE
EEEER
RR
NN!
BLENDY BOY

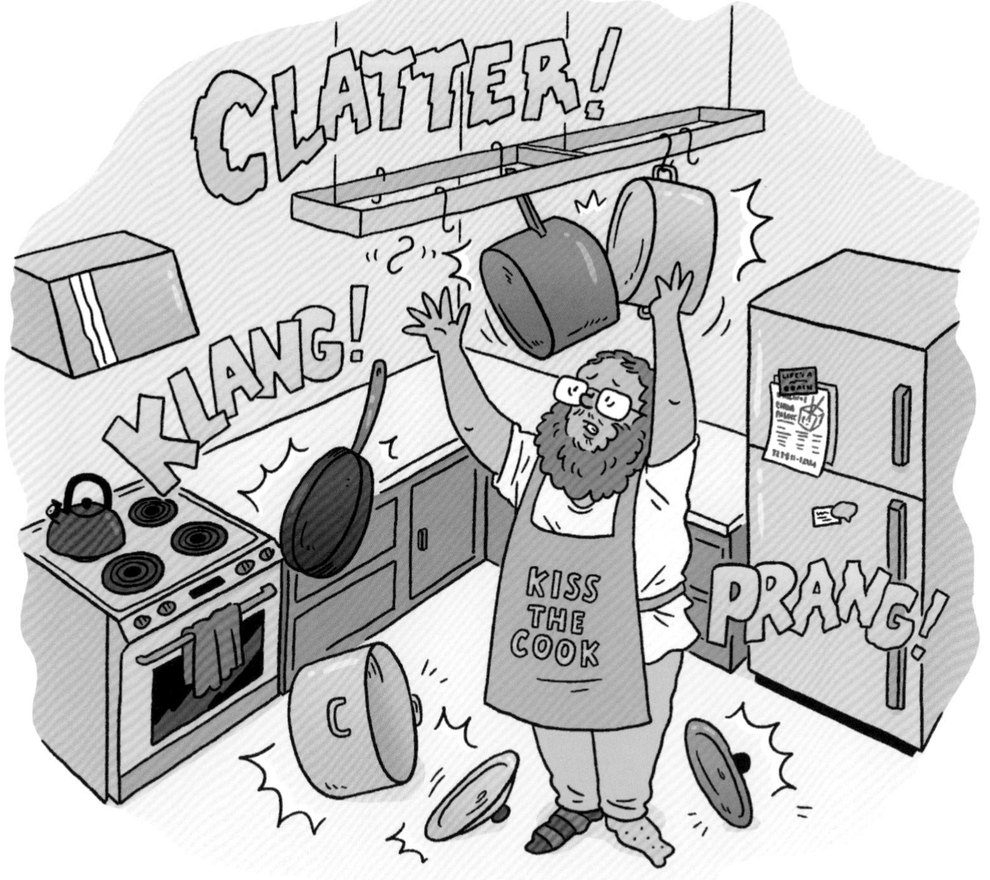
CLATTER!
KLANG!
KISS THE COOK
PRANG!

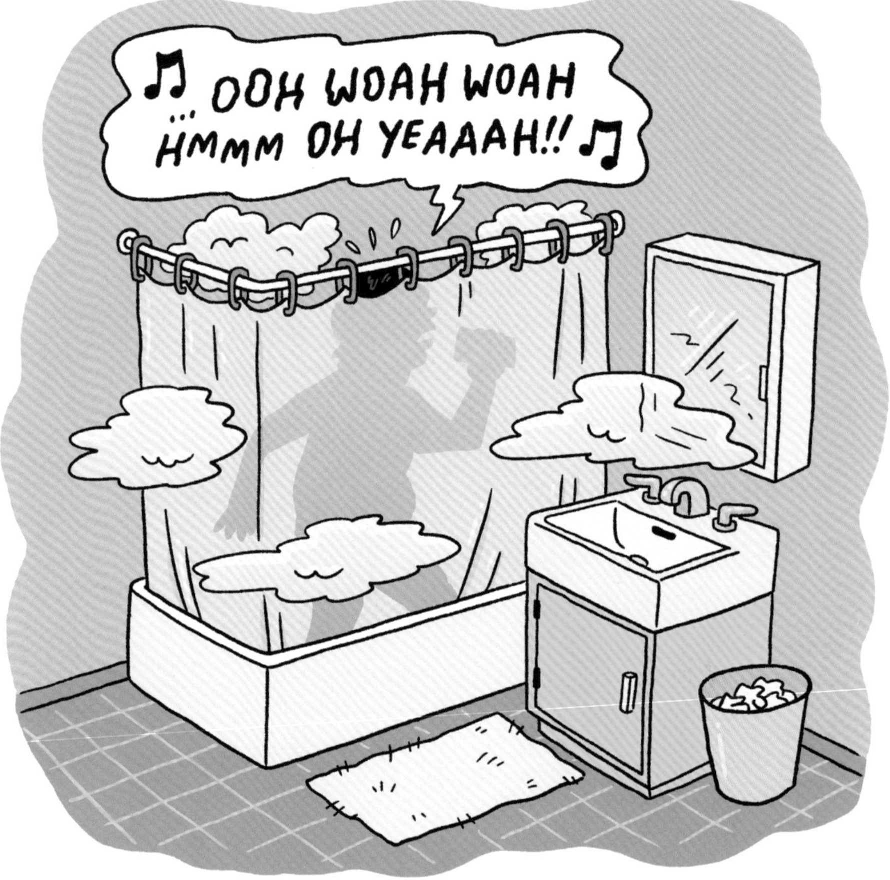
♫ OOH WOAH WOAH ...HMMM OH YEAAAH!! ♫

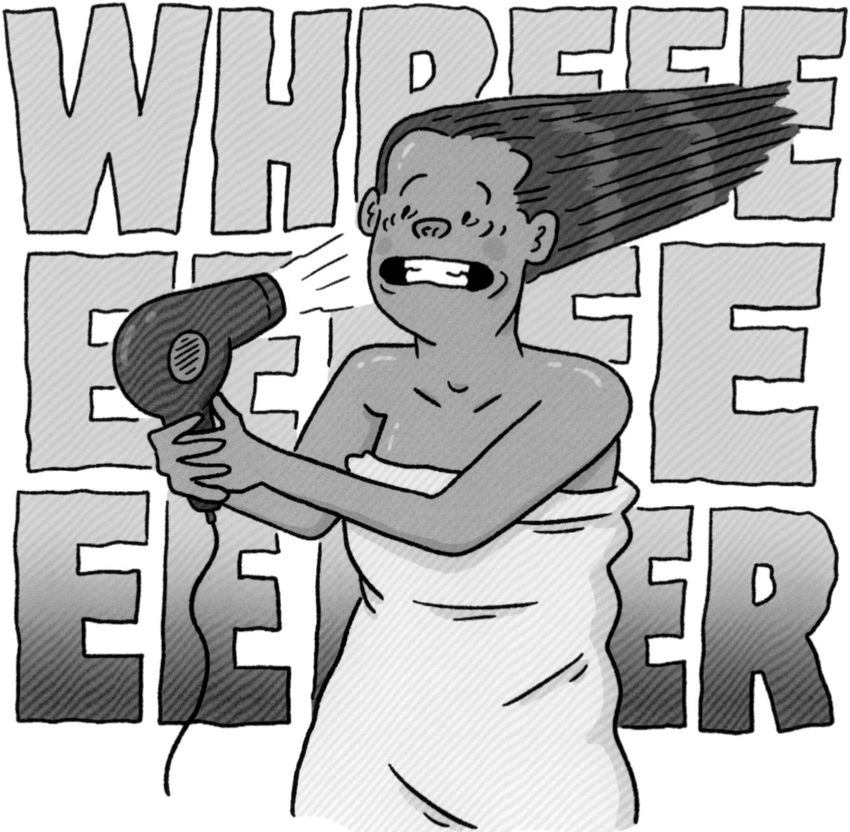
WHEEE
EEEE
EEEER

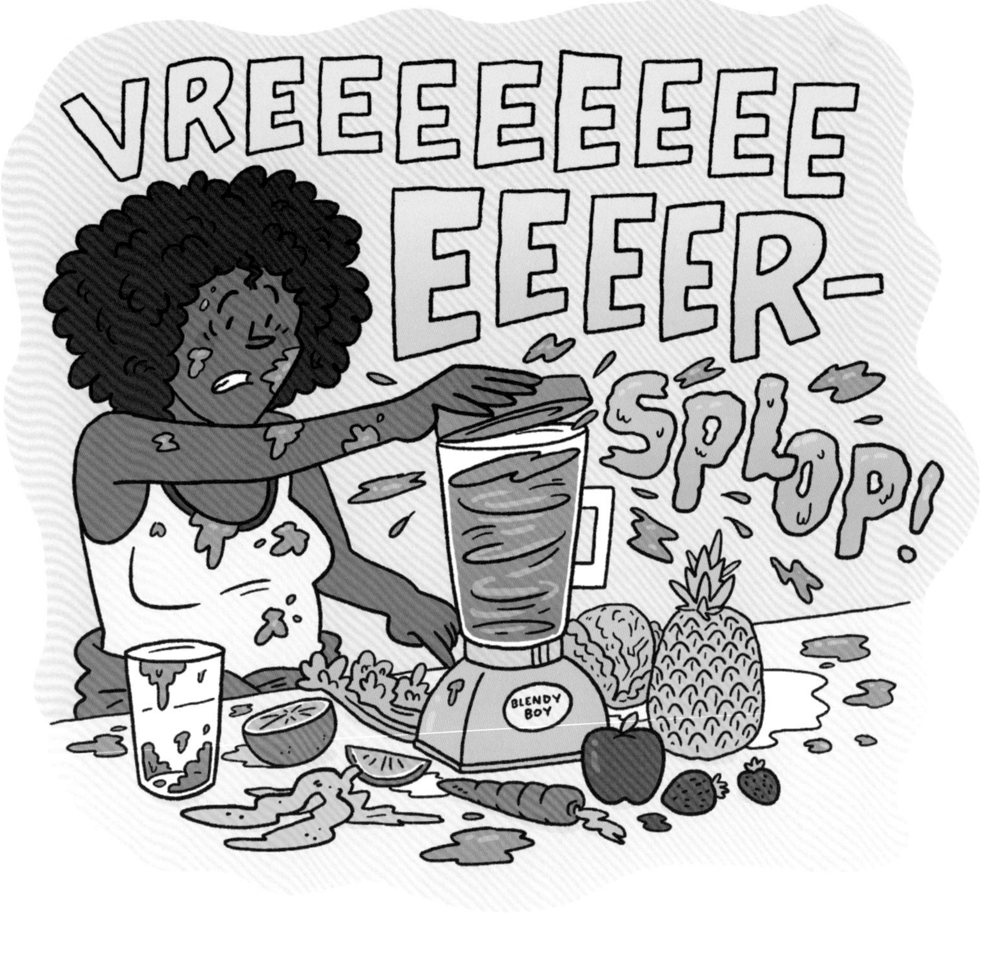
VREEEEEEEEE
EEEER-
SPLOP!
BLENDY BOY

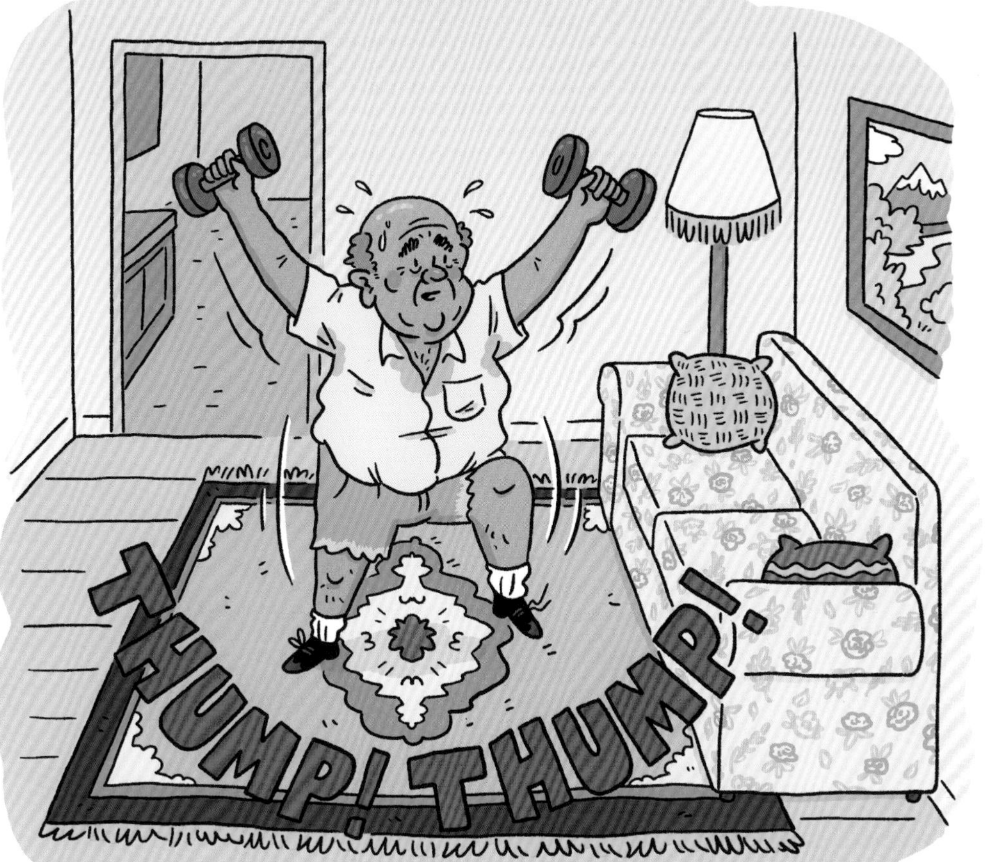
THUMP! THUMP!

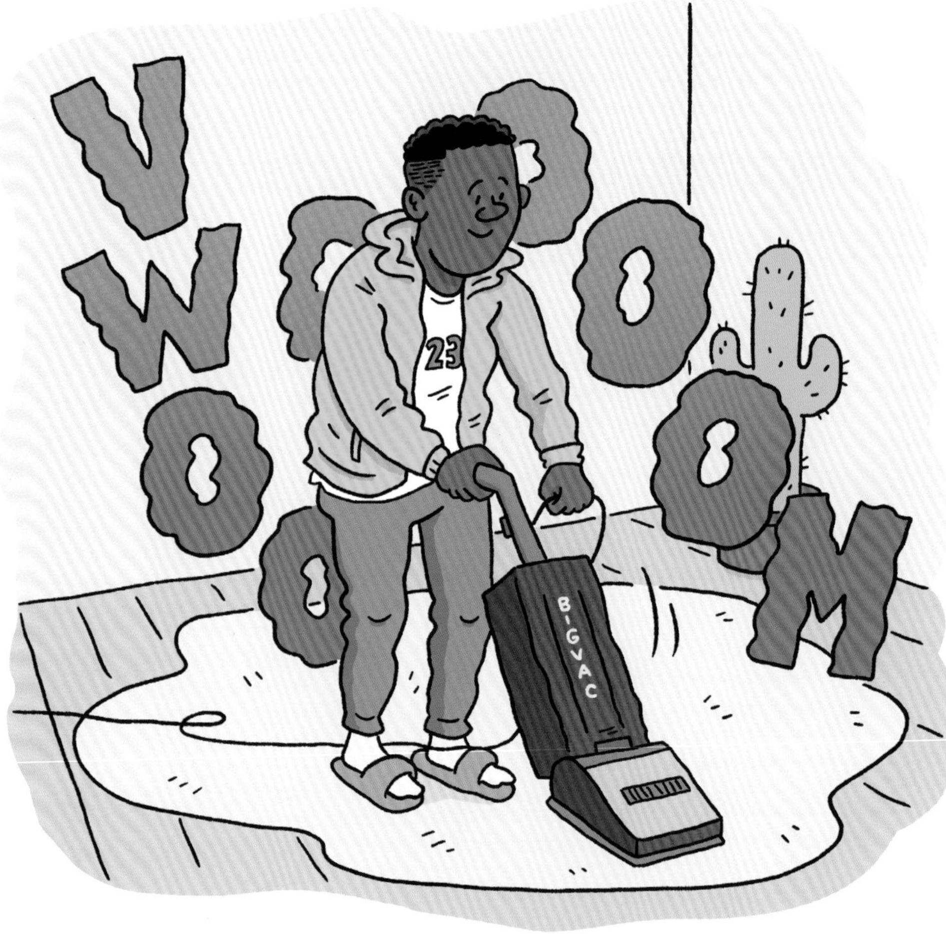
VWOOOOOOM
23
BIGVAC

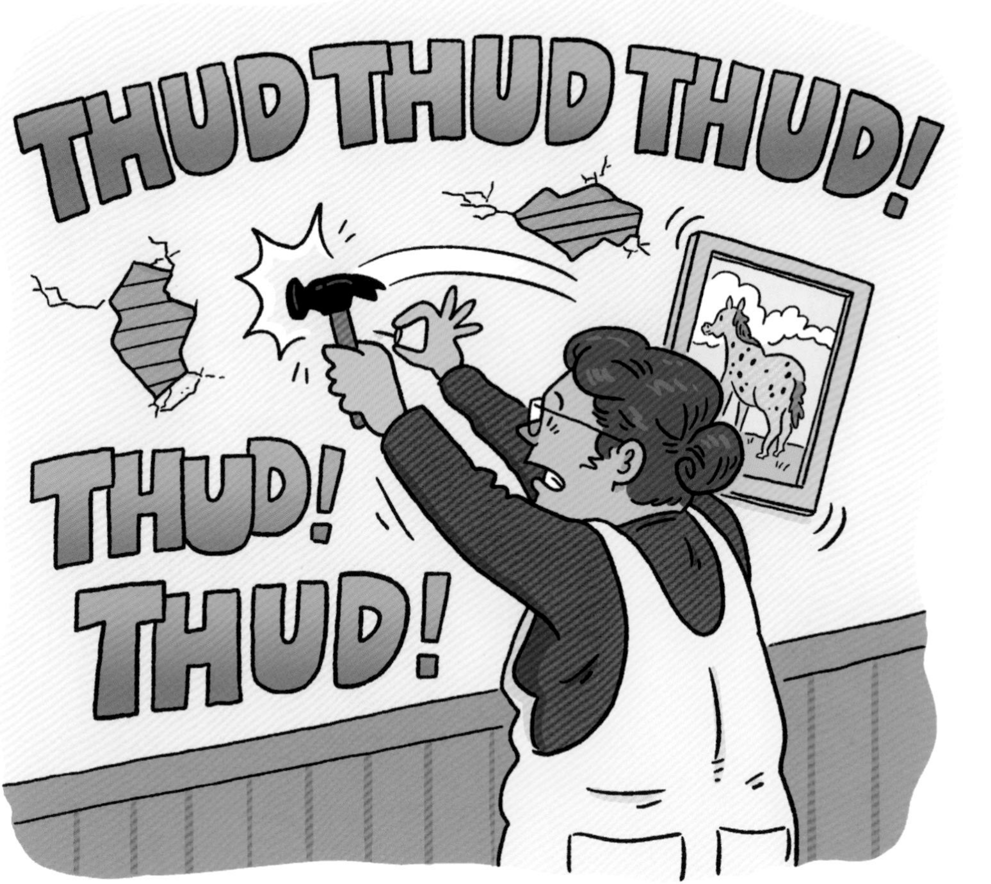
THUD THUD THUD!
THUD!
THUD!

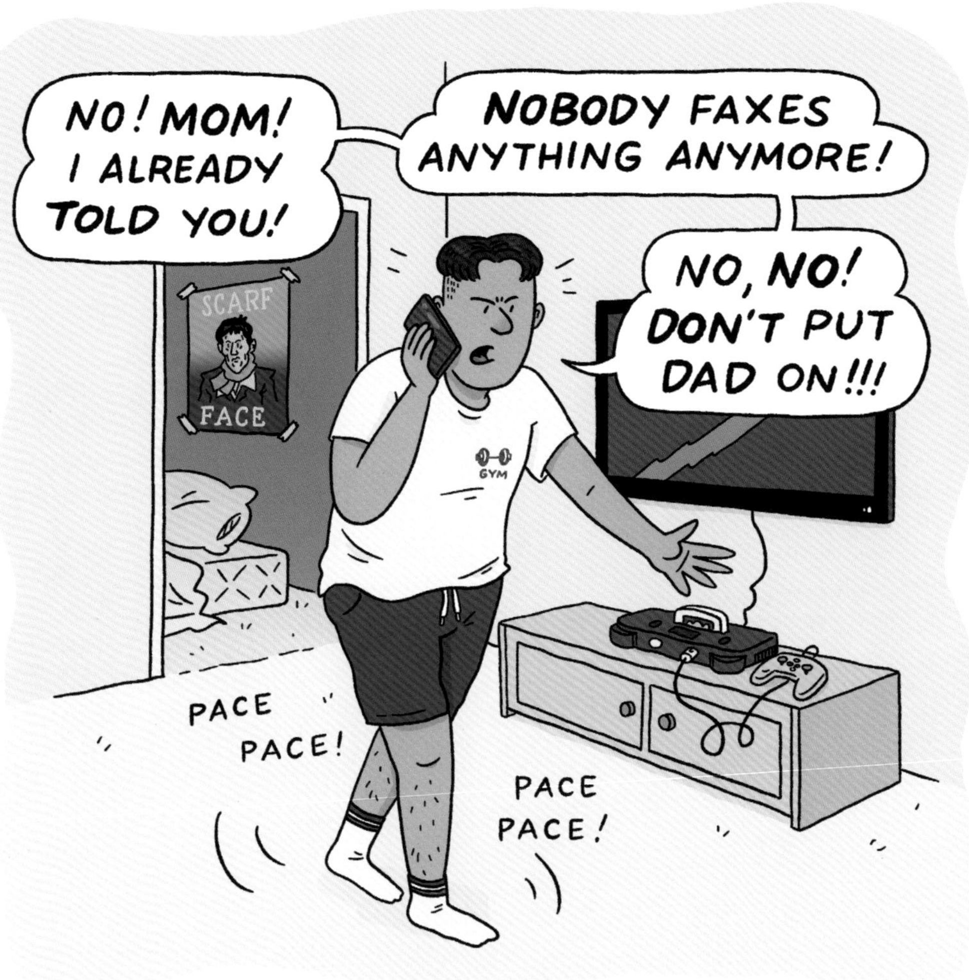
NO! MOM! I ALREADY TOLD YOU!
NOBODY FAXES ANYTHING ANYMORE!
NO, NO! DON'T PUT DAD ON!!!
SCARF FACE
GYM
PACE PACE!
PACE PACE!

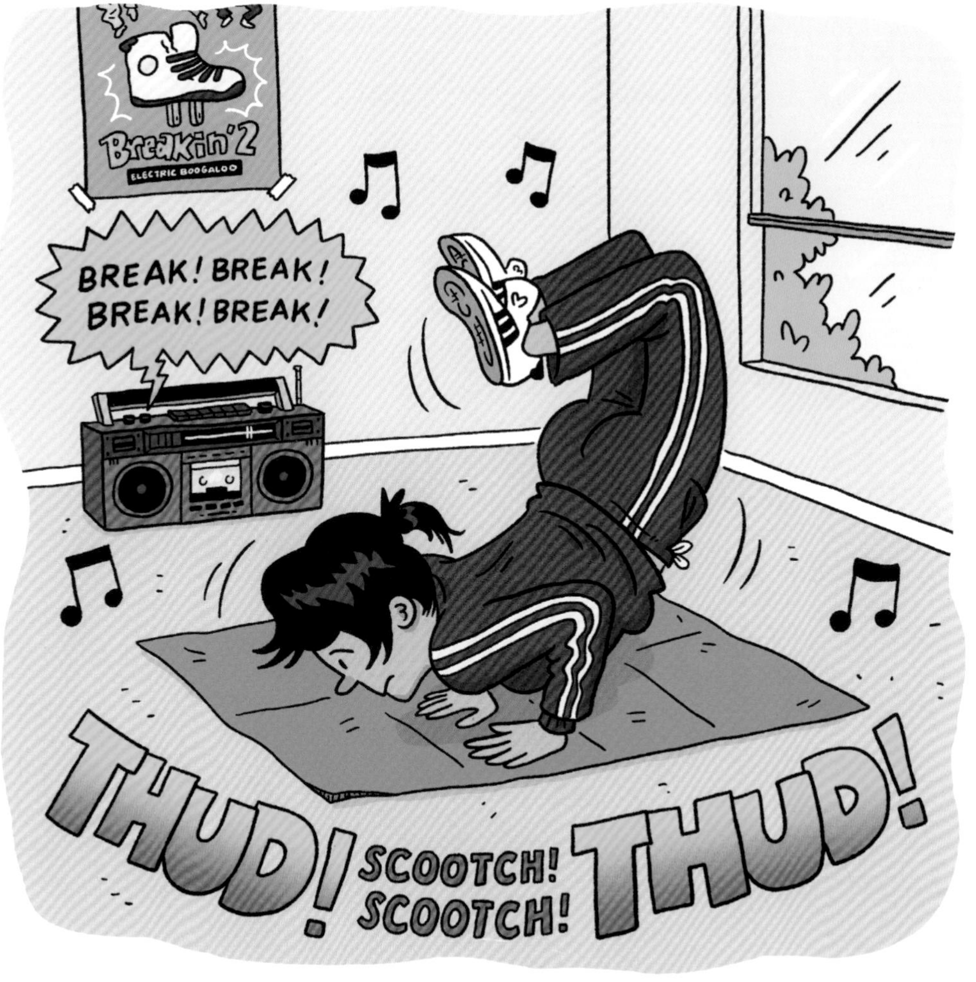
Breakin' 2
ELECTRIC BOOGALOO
BREAK! BREAK!
BREAK! BREAK!
THUD!
SCOOTCH!
SCOOTCH!
THUD!

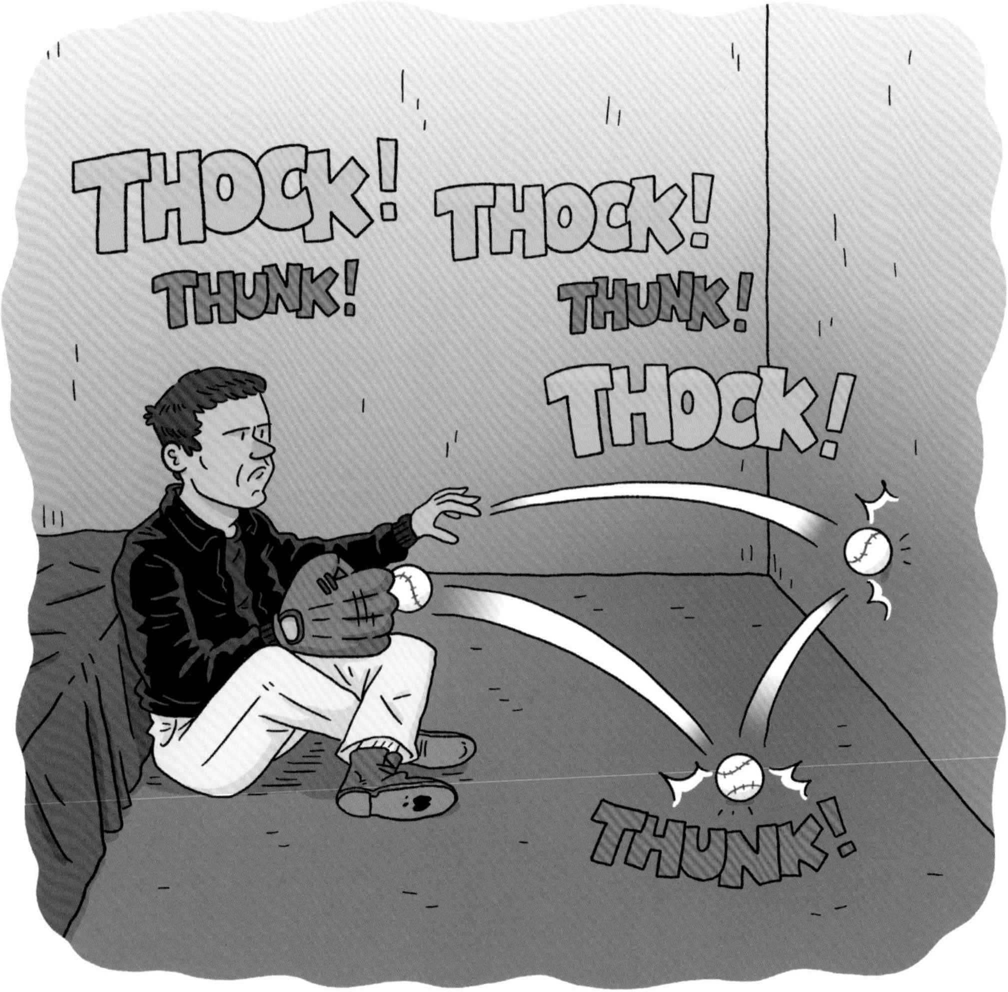
THOCK!
THUNK!
THOCK!
THUNK!
THOCK!
THUNK!

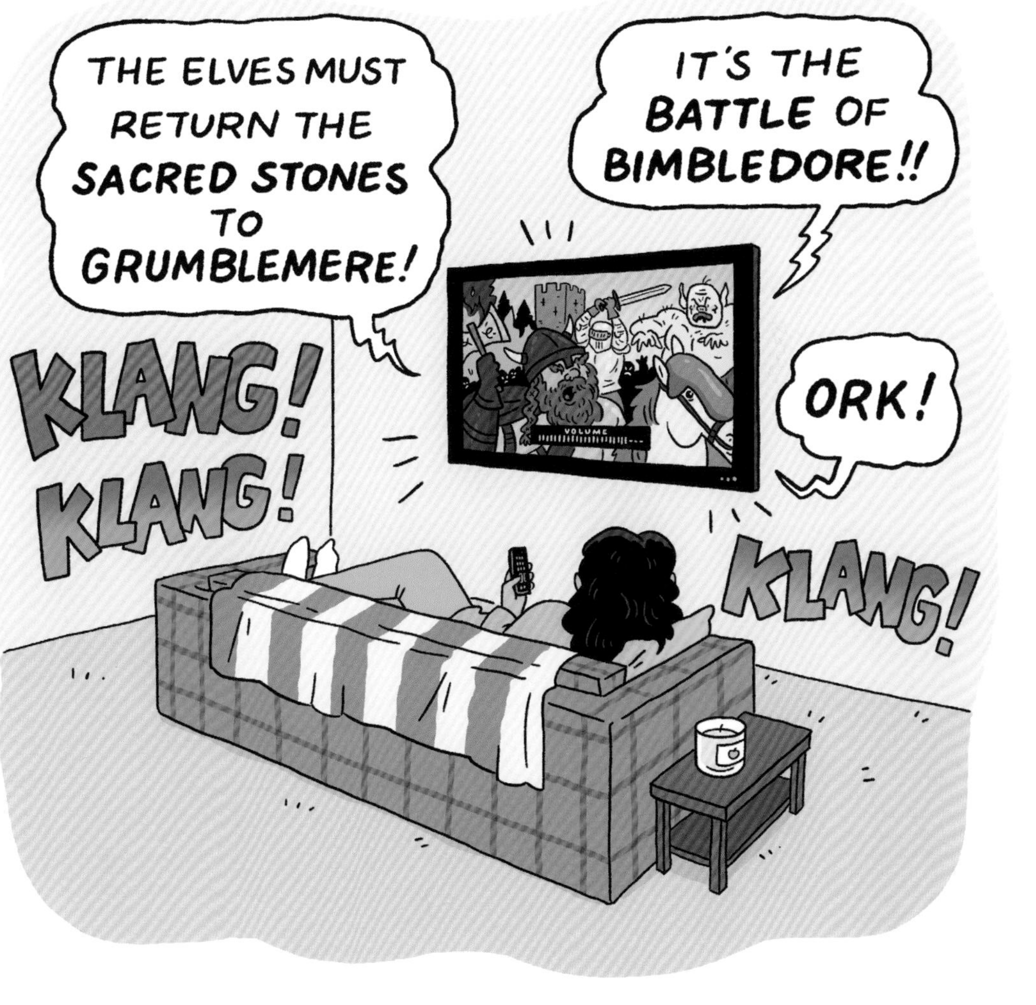
THE ELVES MUST RETURN THE SACRED STONES TO GRUMBLEMERE!
IT'S THE BATTLE OF BIMBLEDORE!!
KLANG! KLANG!
ORK!
KLANG!
VOLUME

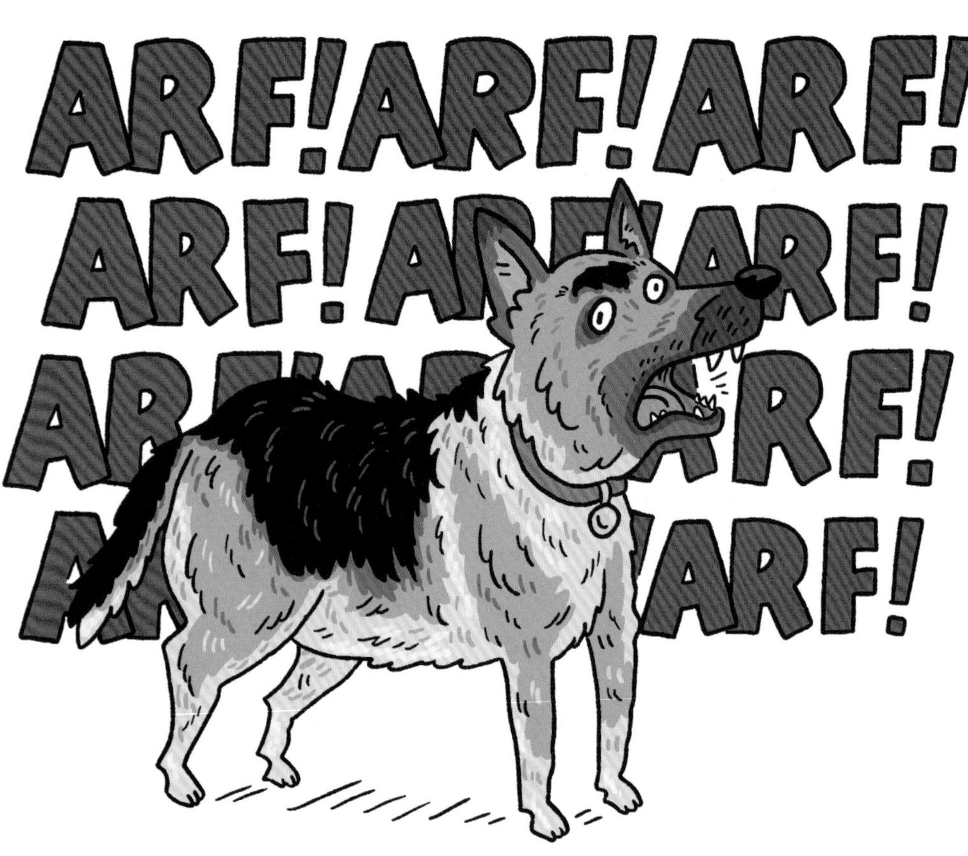
ARF! ARF! ARF!
ARF! ARF!
ARF!
ARF!

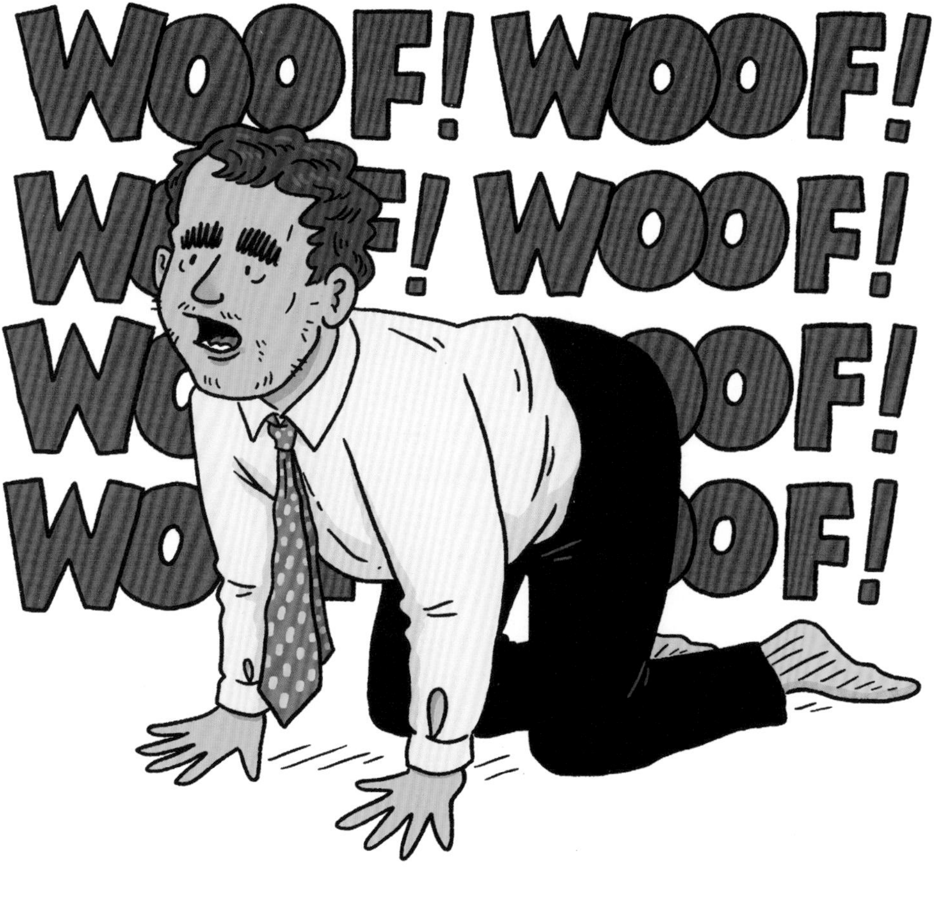
WOOF! WOOF!
WOOF!

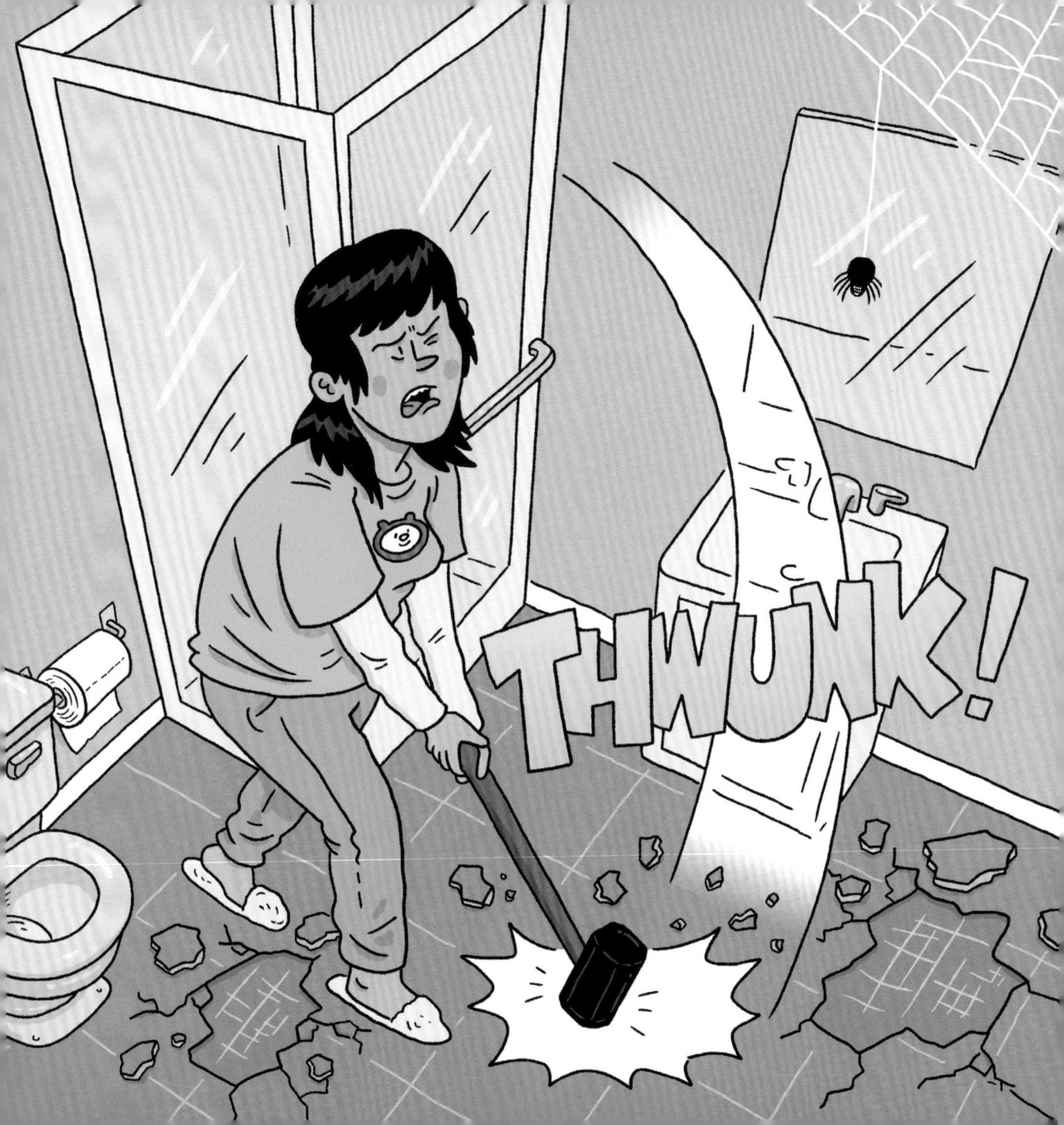
THWUNK!

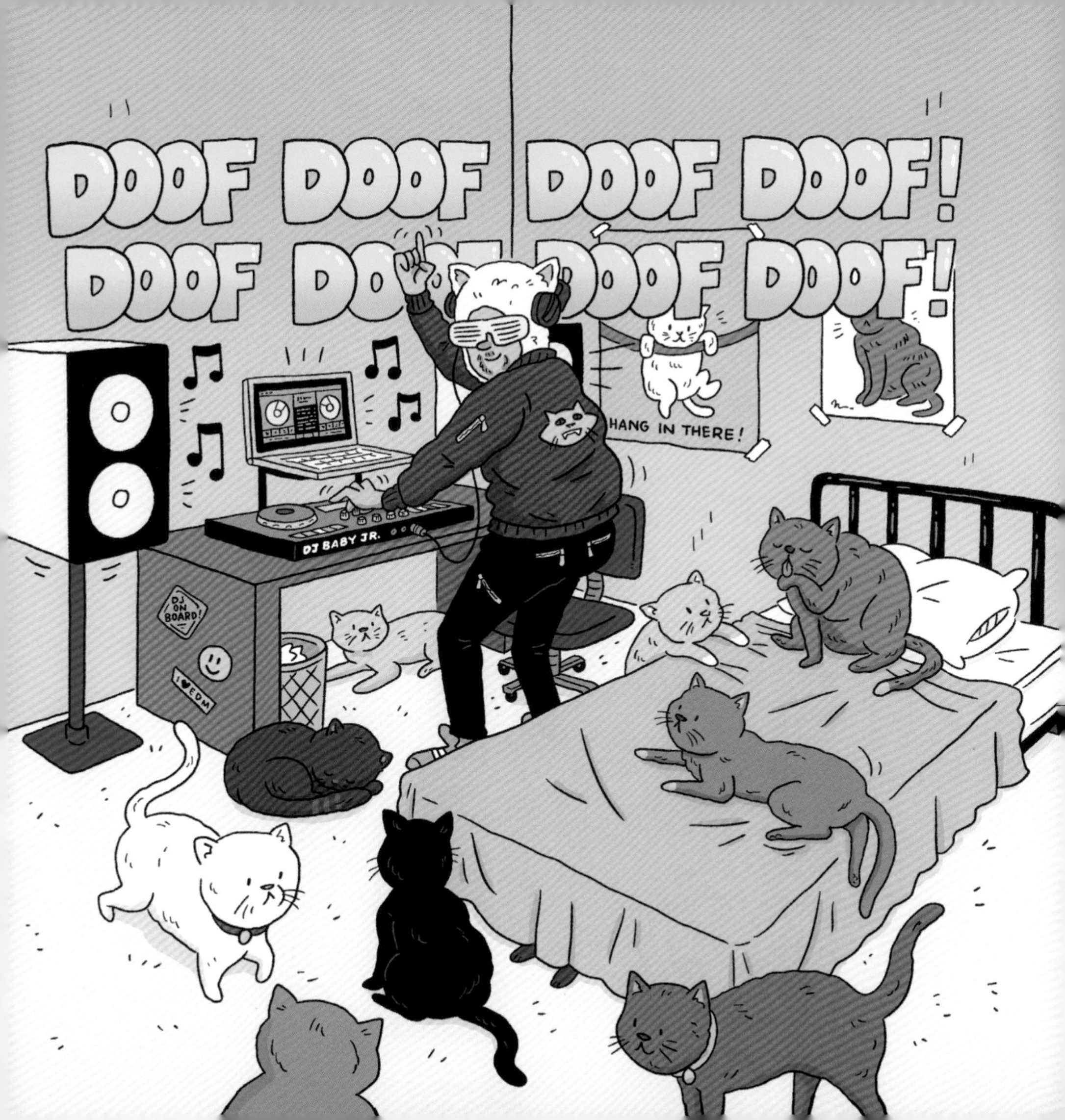
DOOF DOOF DOOF DOOF!
DOOF DOOF DOOF DOOF!
HANG IN THERE!
DJ BABY JR.
DJ ON BOARD!
I ♥ EDM

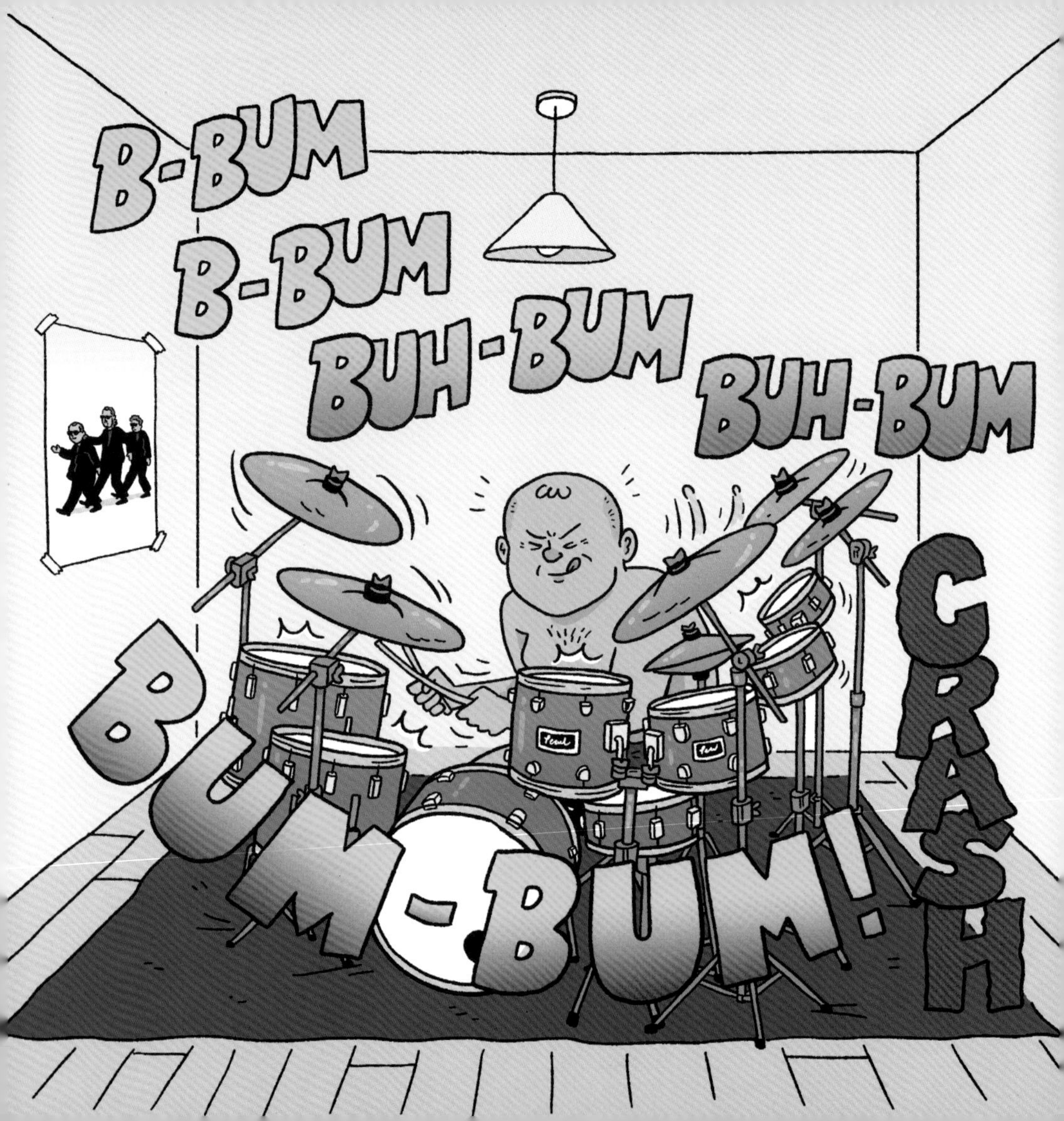
B-BUM
B-BUM
BUH-BUM
BUH-BUM
BUM-BUM!
CRASH

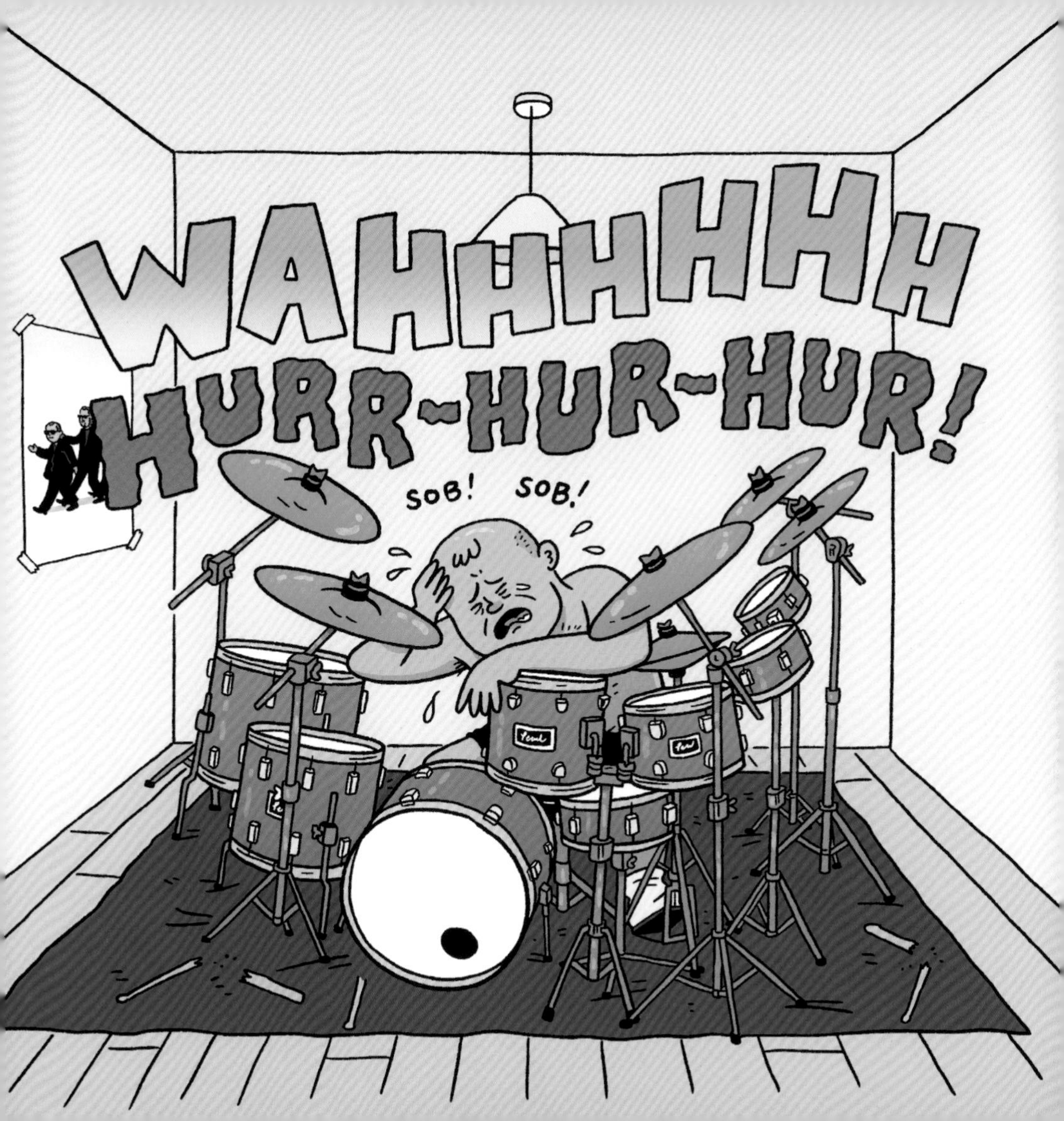
WAHHHHHH
HURR-HUR-HUR!
SOB! SOB!

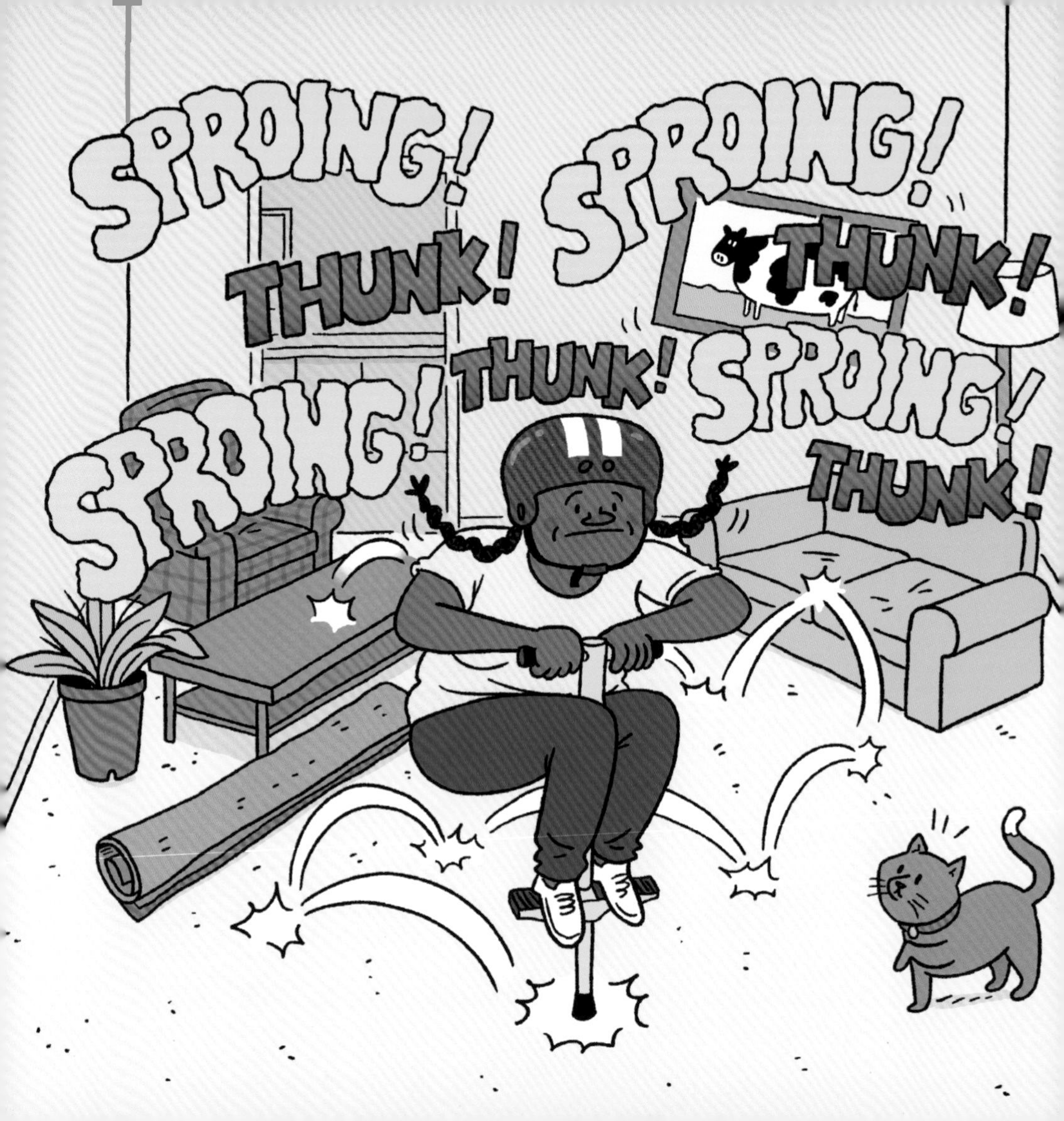
SPROING!
THUNK!
SPROING!
THUNK!
SPROING!
THUNK!
SPROING!
THUNK!

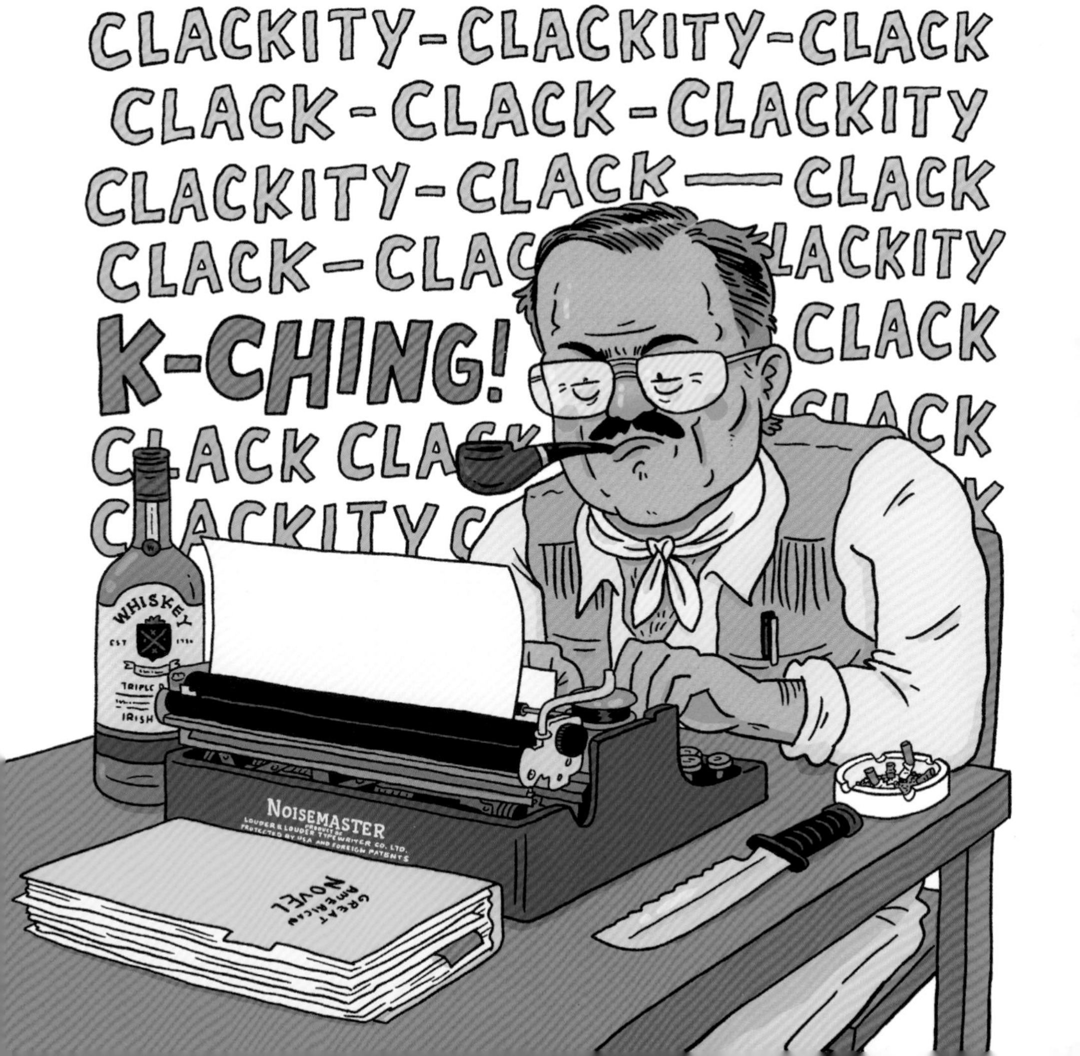

CLACKITY-CLACKITY-CLACK
CLACK-CLACK-CLACKITY
CLACKITY-CLACK—CLACK
CLACK—CLA
LACKITY
K-CHING!
CLACK
ACK
WHISKEY
IRISH
NOISEMASTER
PRODUCT OF
LOUDER & LOUDER TYPEWRITER CO. LTD.
PROTECTED BY USA AND FOREIGN PATENTS
GREAT AMERICAN NOVEL

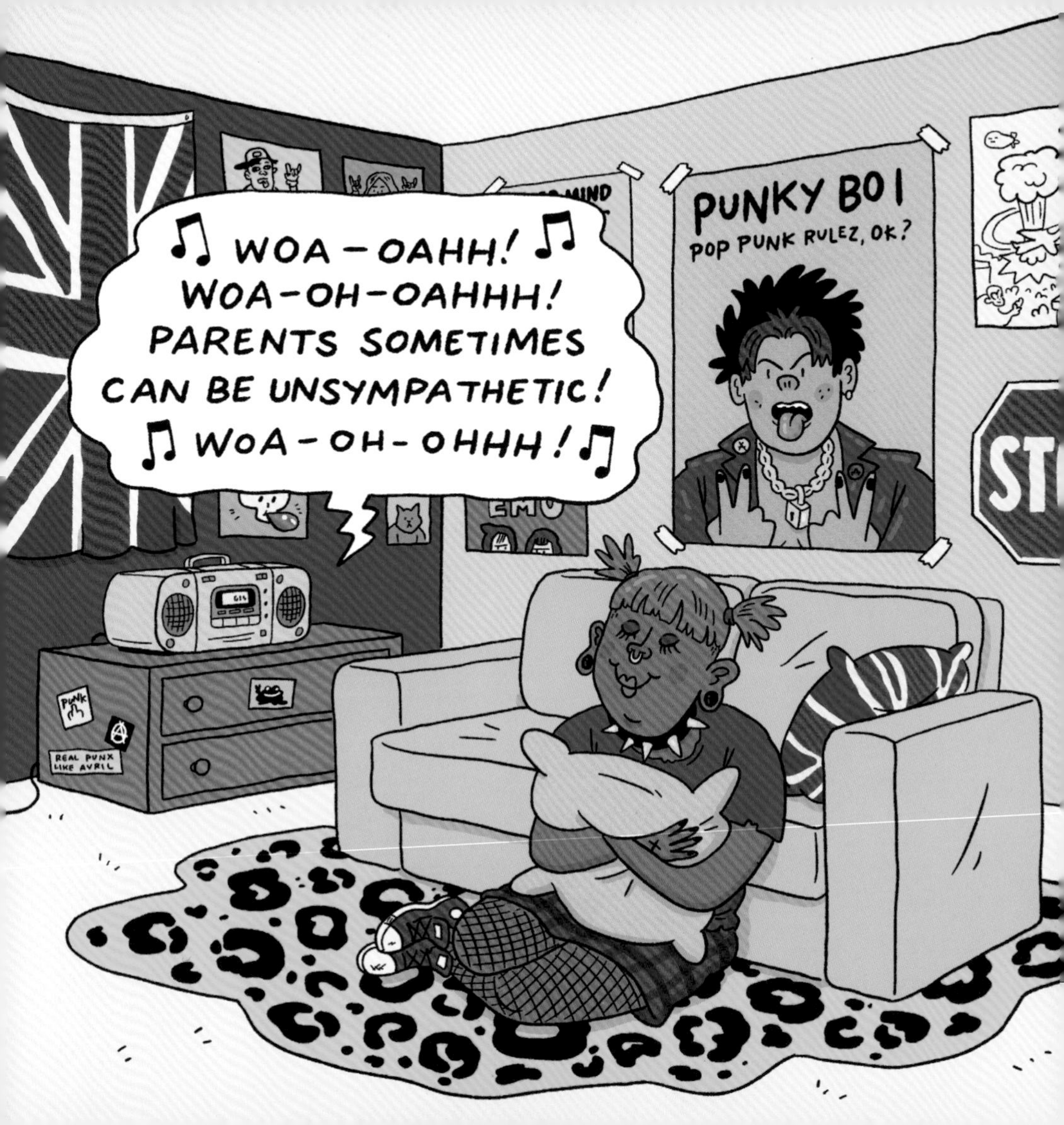
♫ WOA-OAHH! ♫
WOA-OH-OAHHH!
PARENTS SOMETIMES
CAN BE UNSYMPATHETIC!
♫ WOA-OH-OHHH! ♫
PUNKY BOI
POP PUNK RULEZ, OK?
EMO
PUNK
REAL PUNX LIKE AVRIL

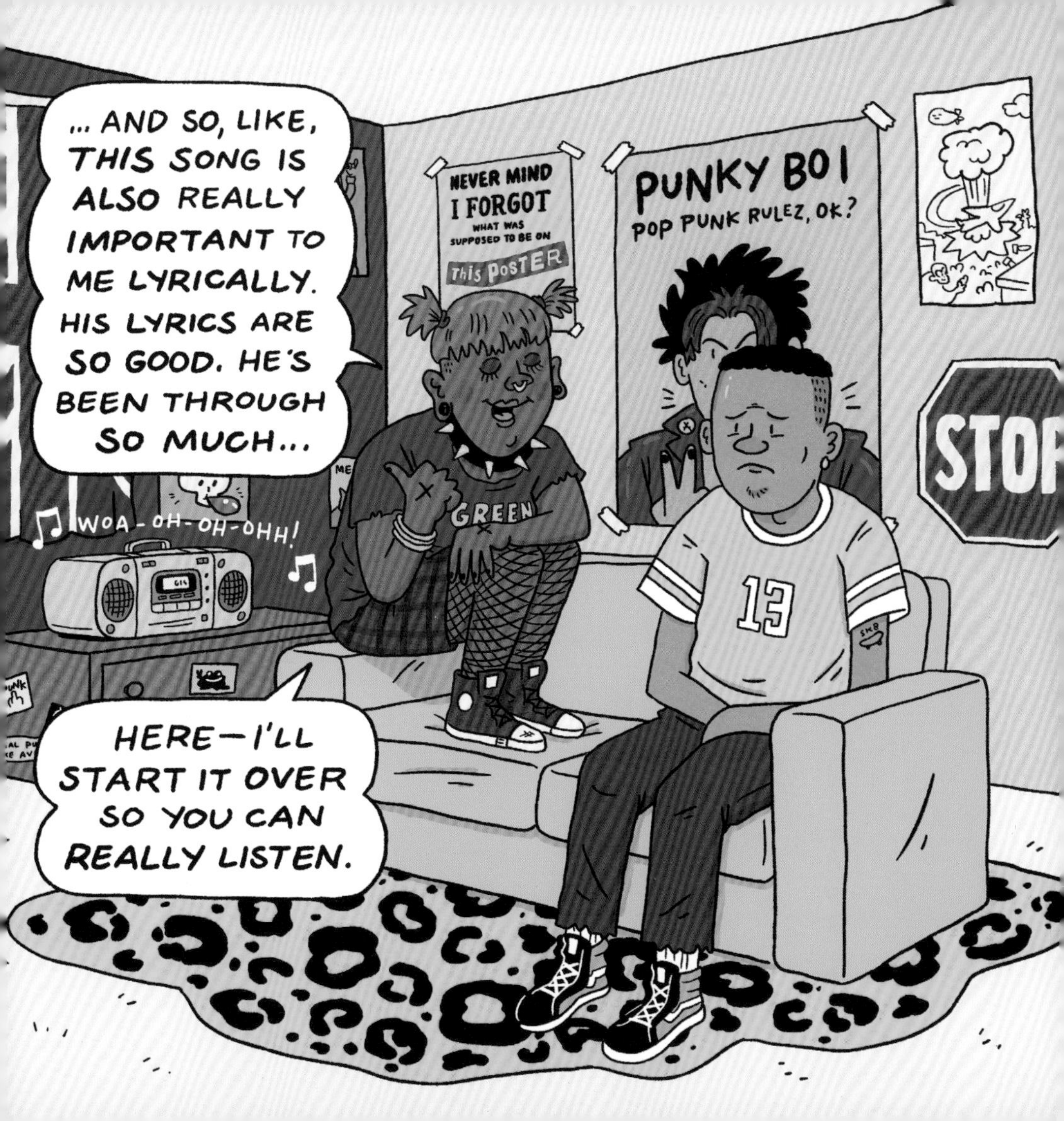

... AND SO, LIKE, THIS SONG IS ALSO REALLY IMPORTANT TO ME LYRICALLY. HIS LYRICS ARE SO GOOD. HE'S BEEN THROUGH SO MUCH...
NEVER MIND I FORGOT WHAT WAS SUPPOSED TO BE ON This POSTER
PUNKY BOI
POP PUNK RULEZ, OK?
STOP
WOA-OH-OH-OHH!
GREEN
13
SKB
HERE—I'LL START IT OVER SO YOU CAN REALLY LISTEN.

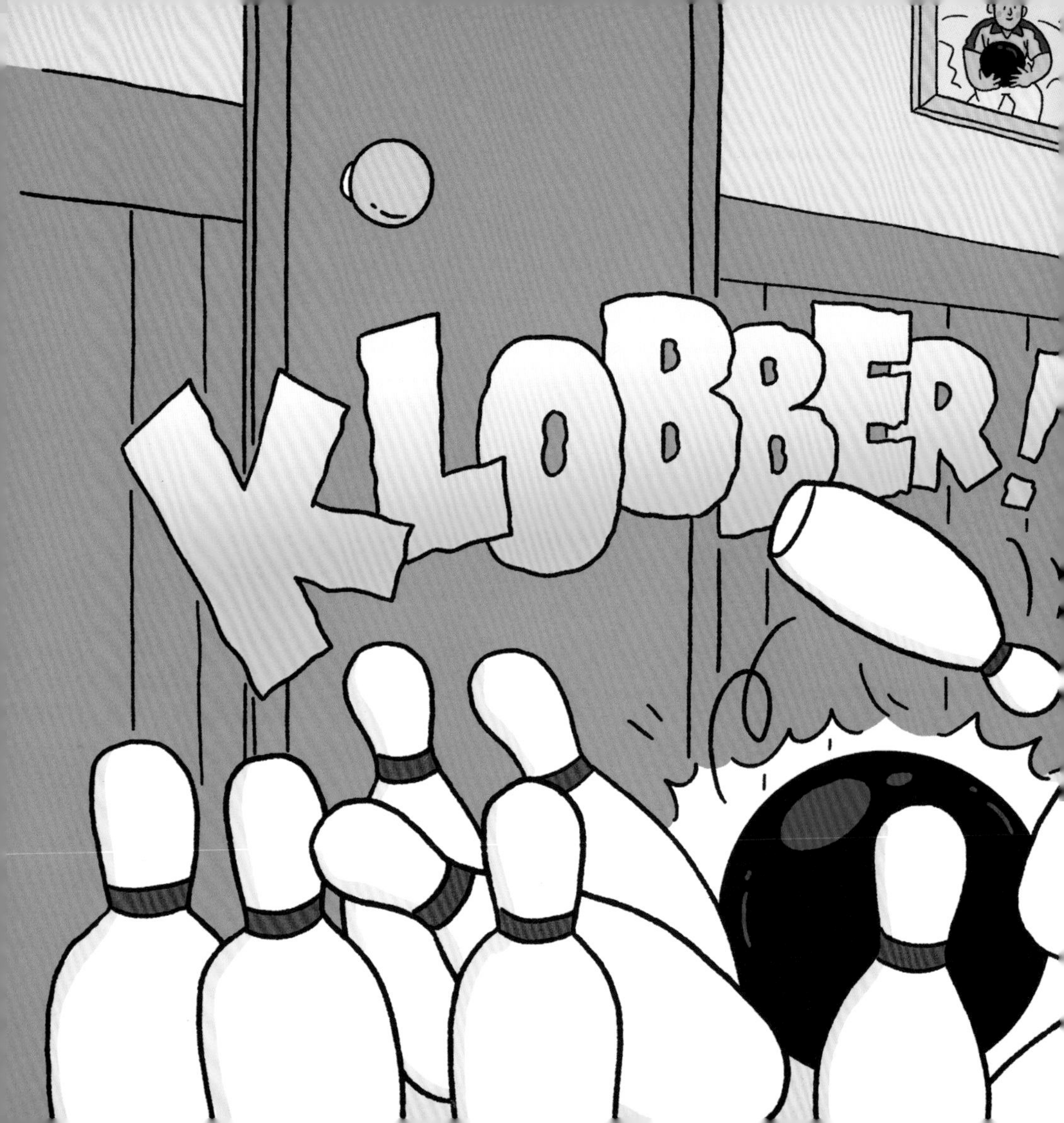
KLOBBER!

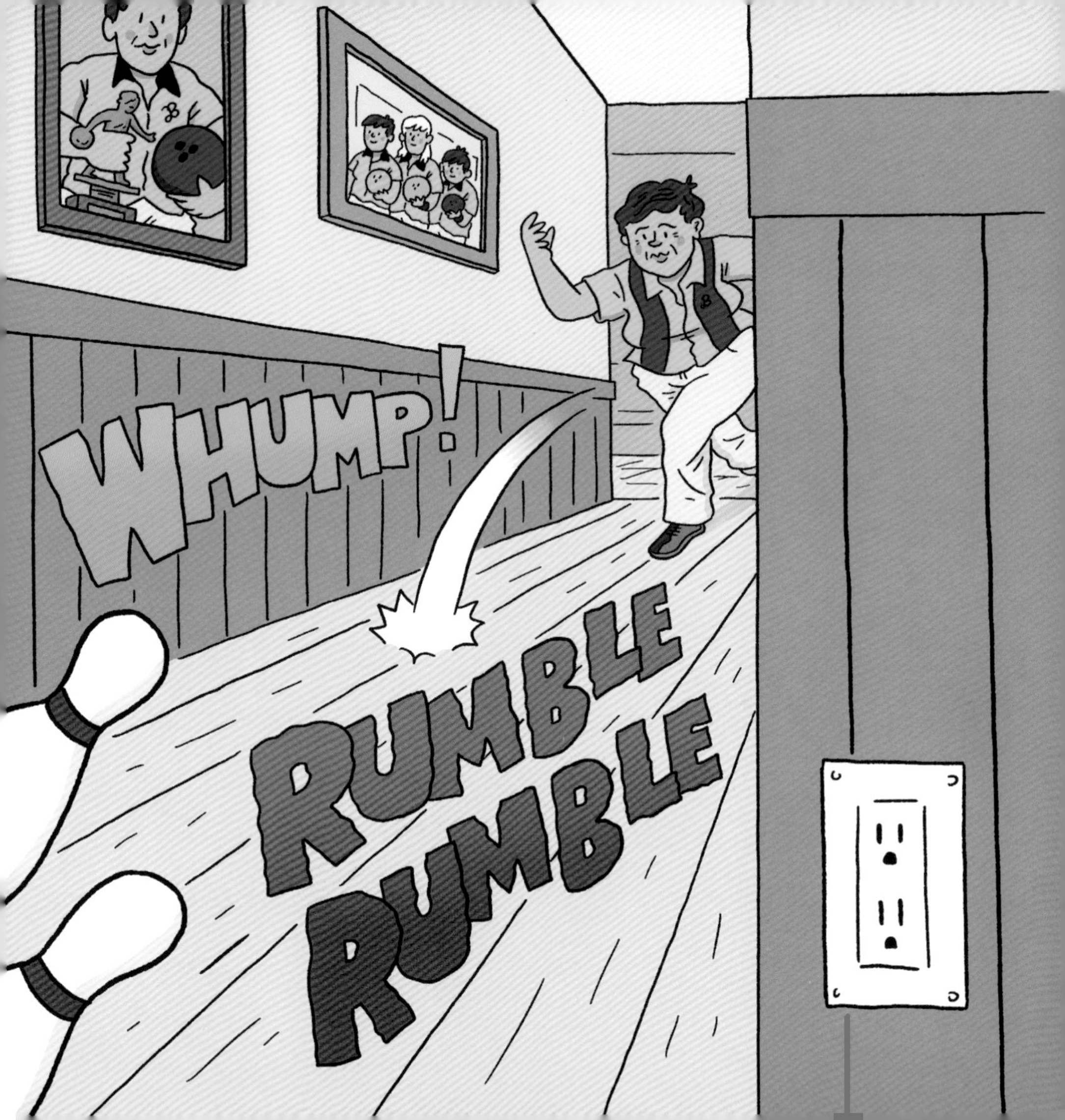
WHUMP!
RUMBLE
RUMBLE

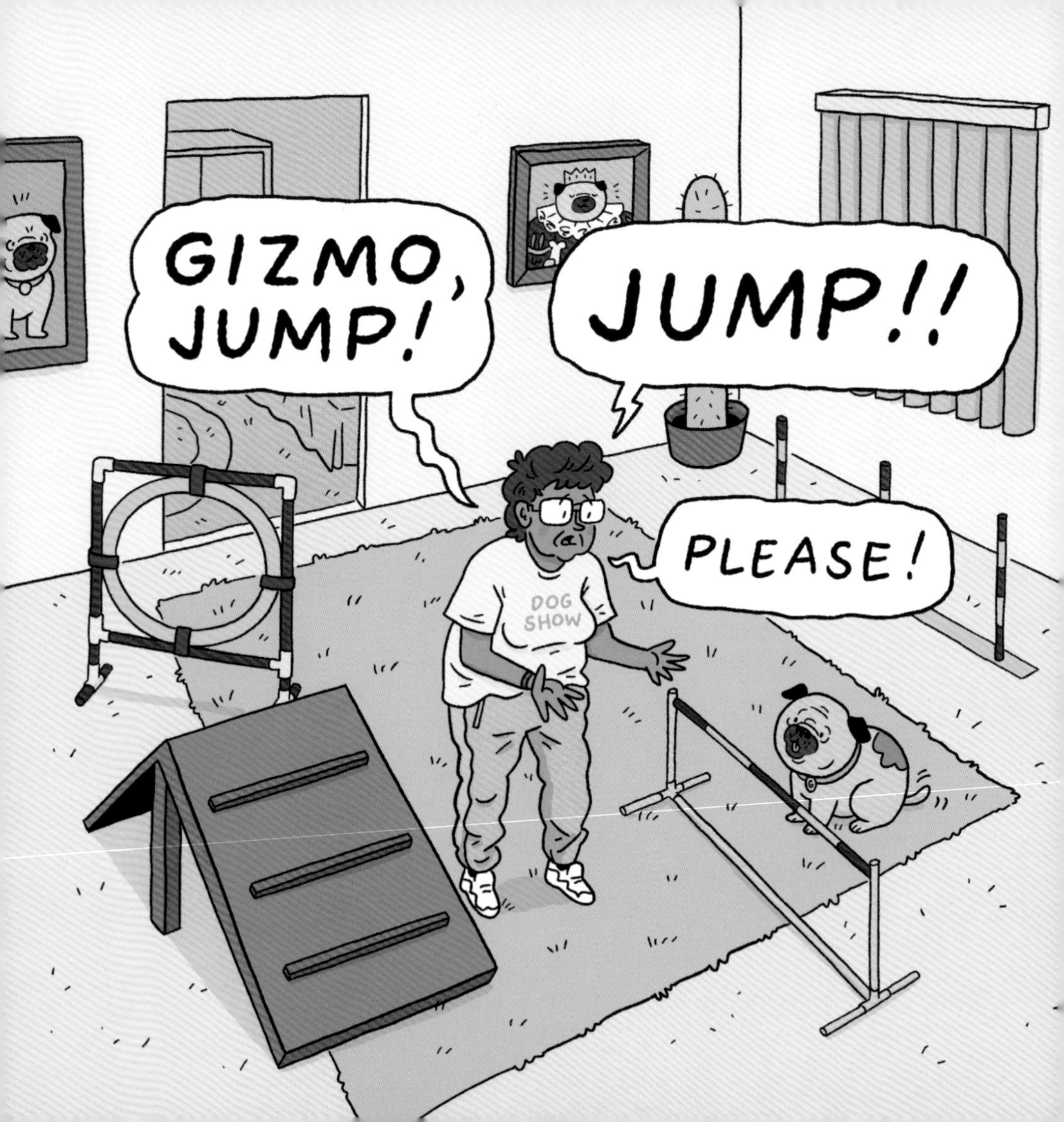

GIZMO, JUMP!
JUMP!!
PLEASE!
DOG SHOW

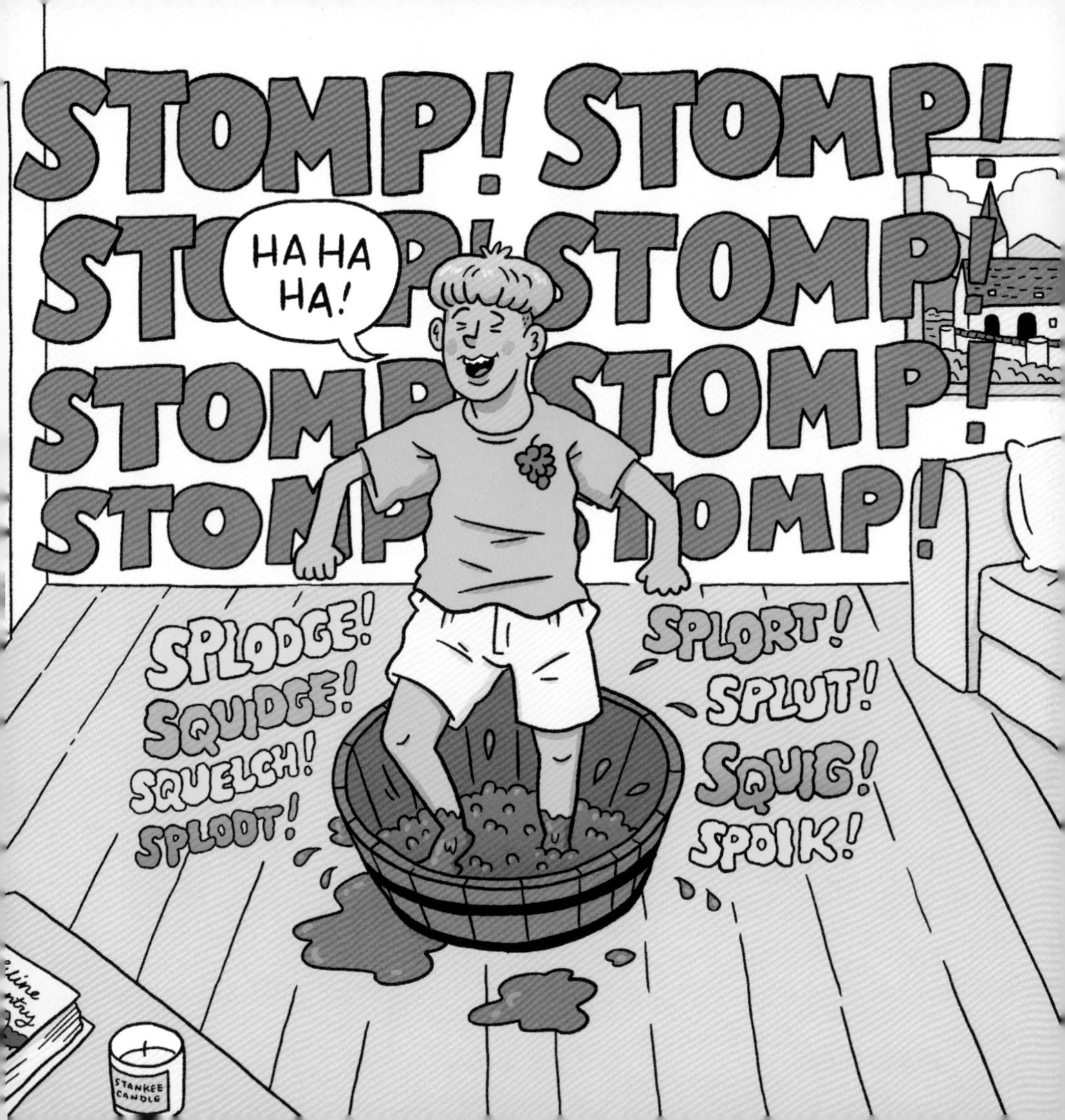
STOMP! STOMP!
STOMP!
STOMP!
HA HA HA!
SPLODGE!
SQUIDGE!
SQUELCH!
SPLOOT!
SPLORT!
SPLUT!
SQUIG!
SPOIK!
STANKEE CANDLE

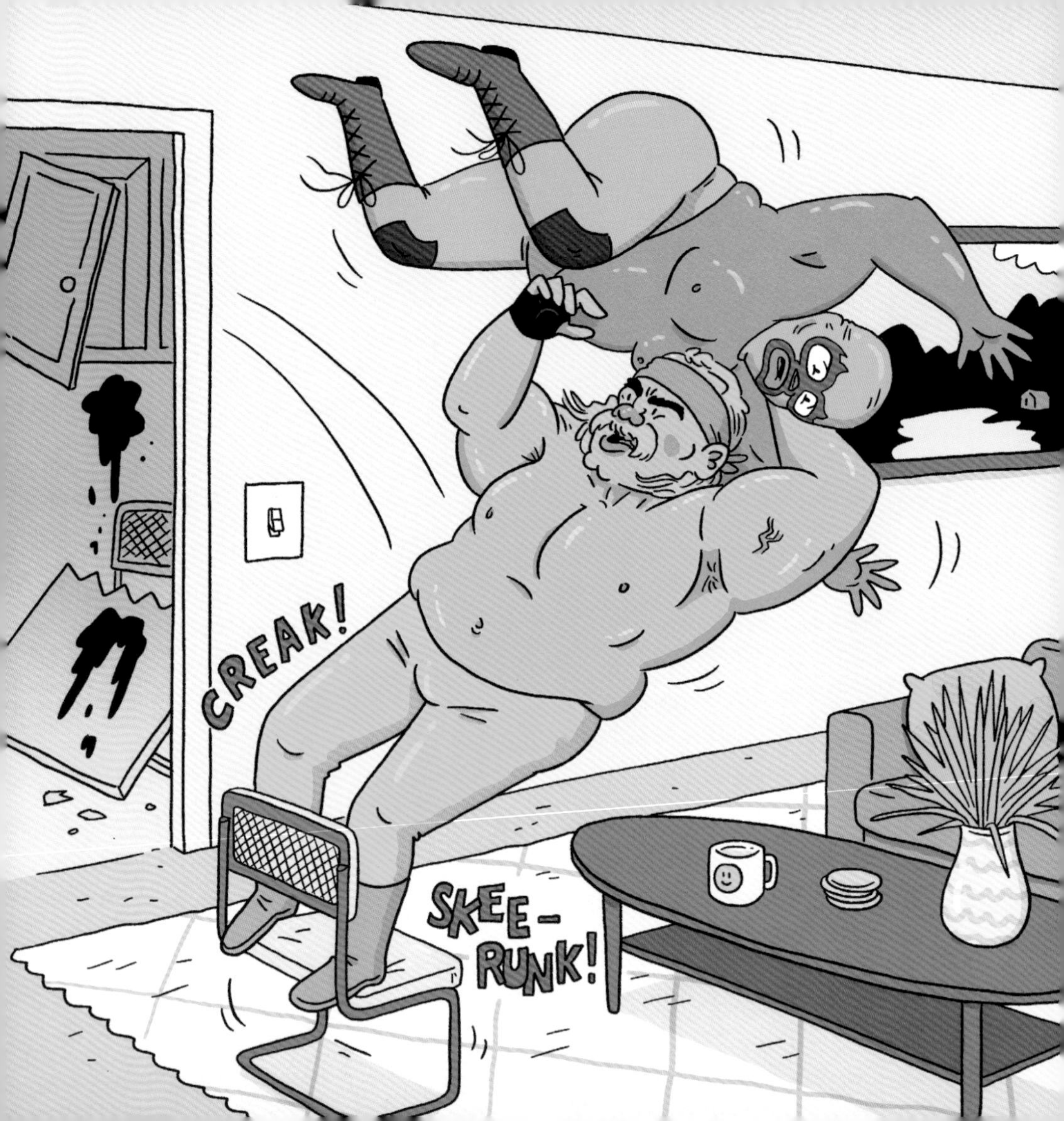
CREAK!
SKEE-
RUNK!

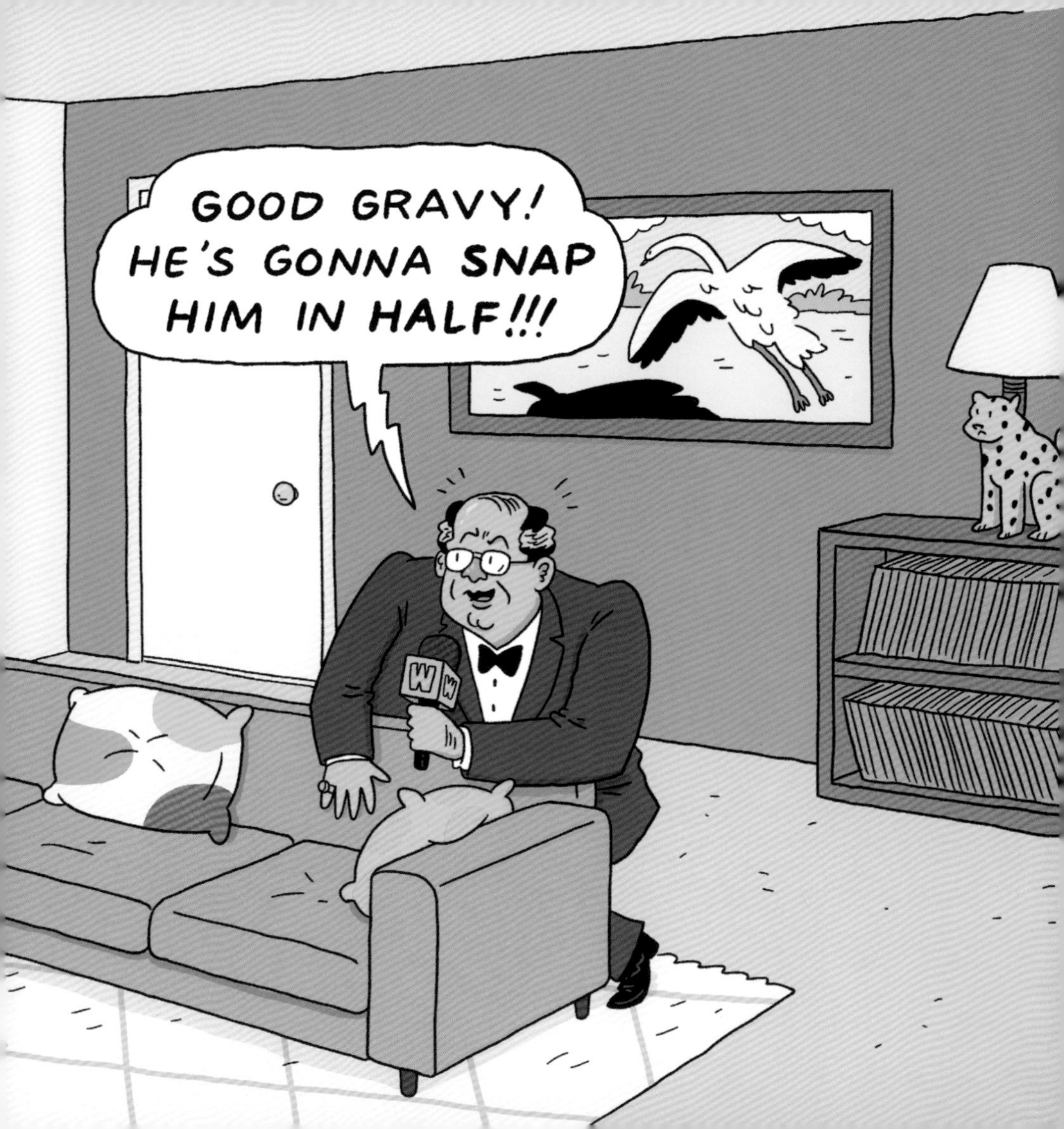
GOOD GRAVY! HE'S GONNA SNAP HIM IN HALF!!!
W W

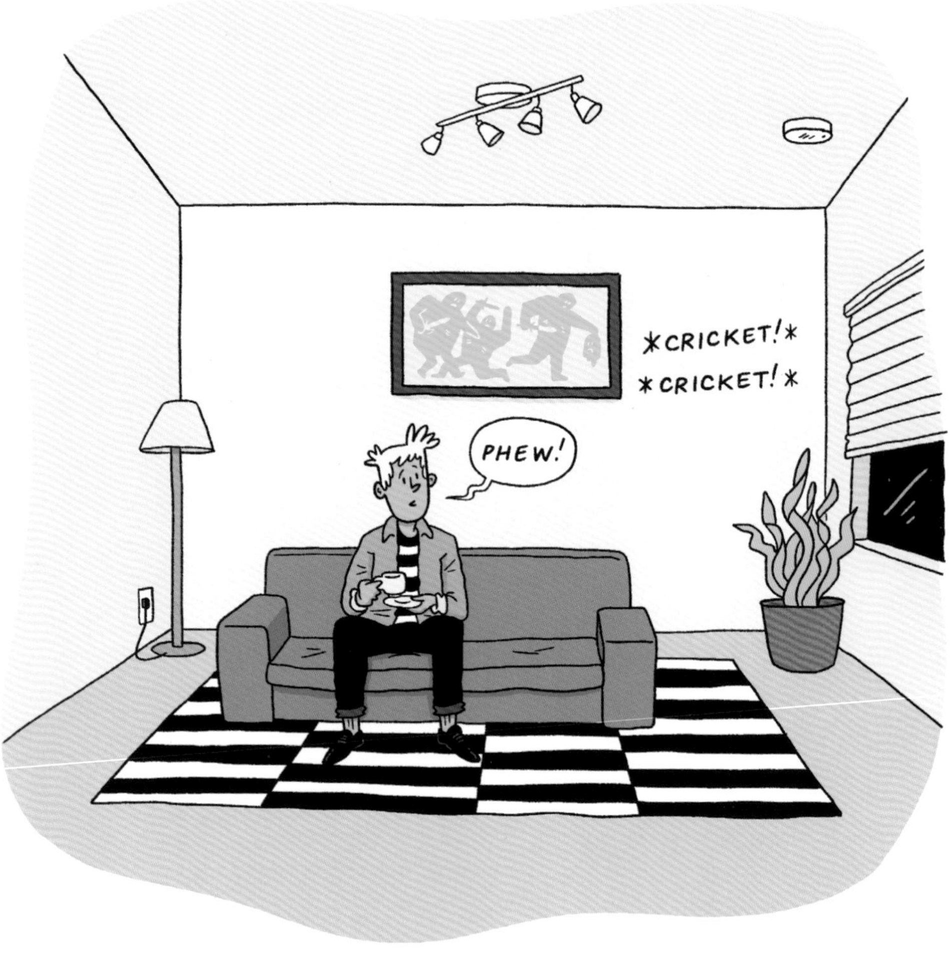
CRICKET!
CRICKET!
PHEW!

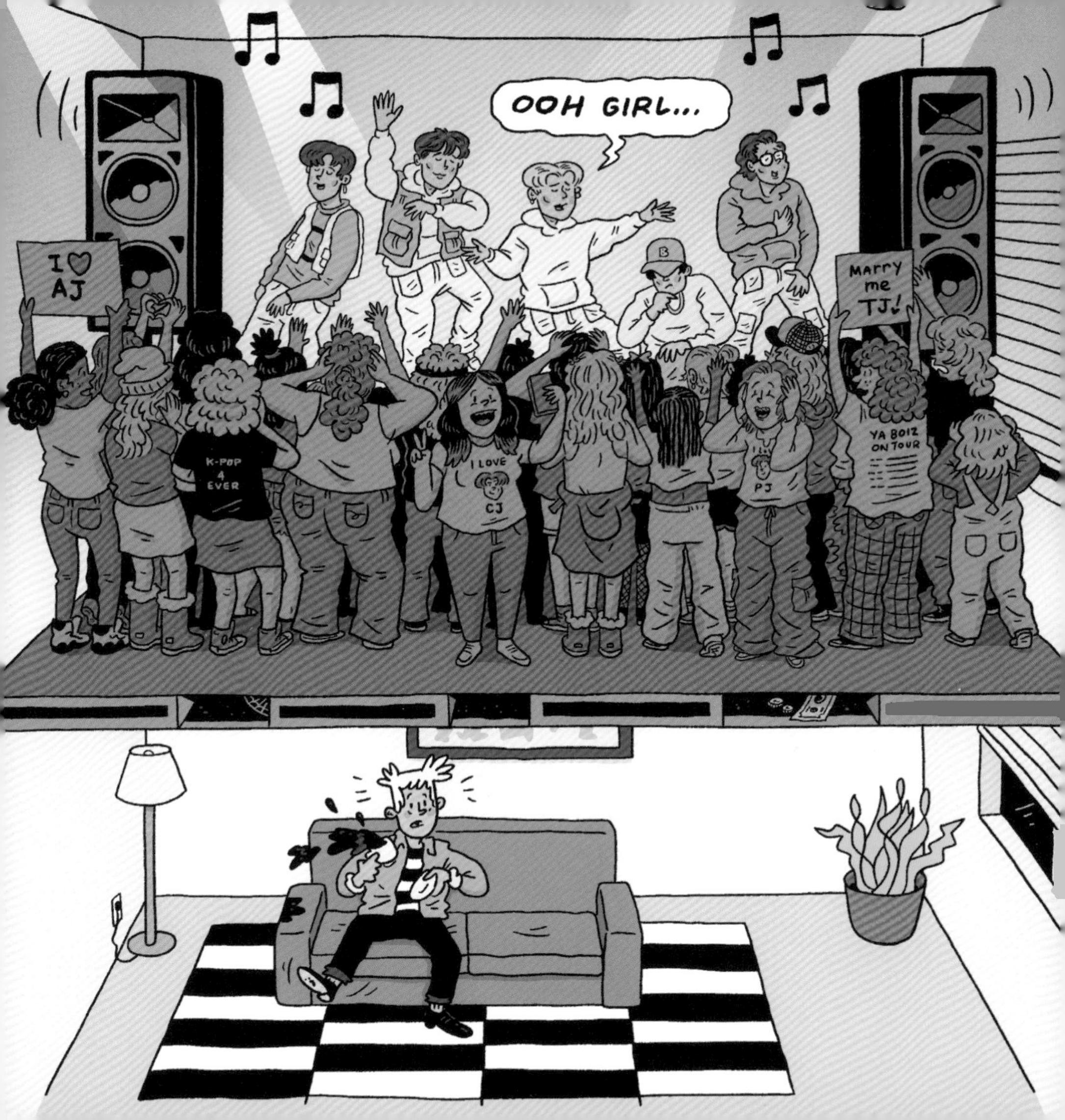
OOH GIRL...
I ♥ AJ
Marry me TJ!
K-POP 4 EVER
I LOVE CJ
PJ
YA BOIZ ON TOUR

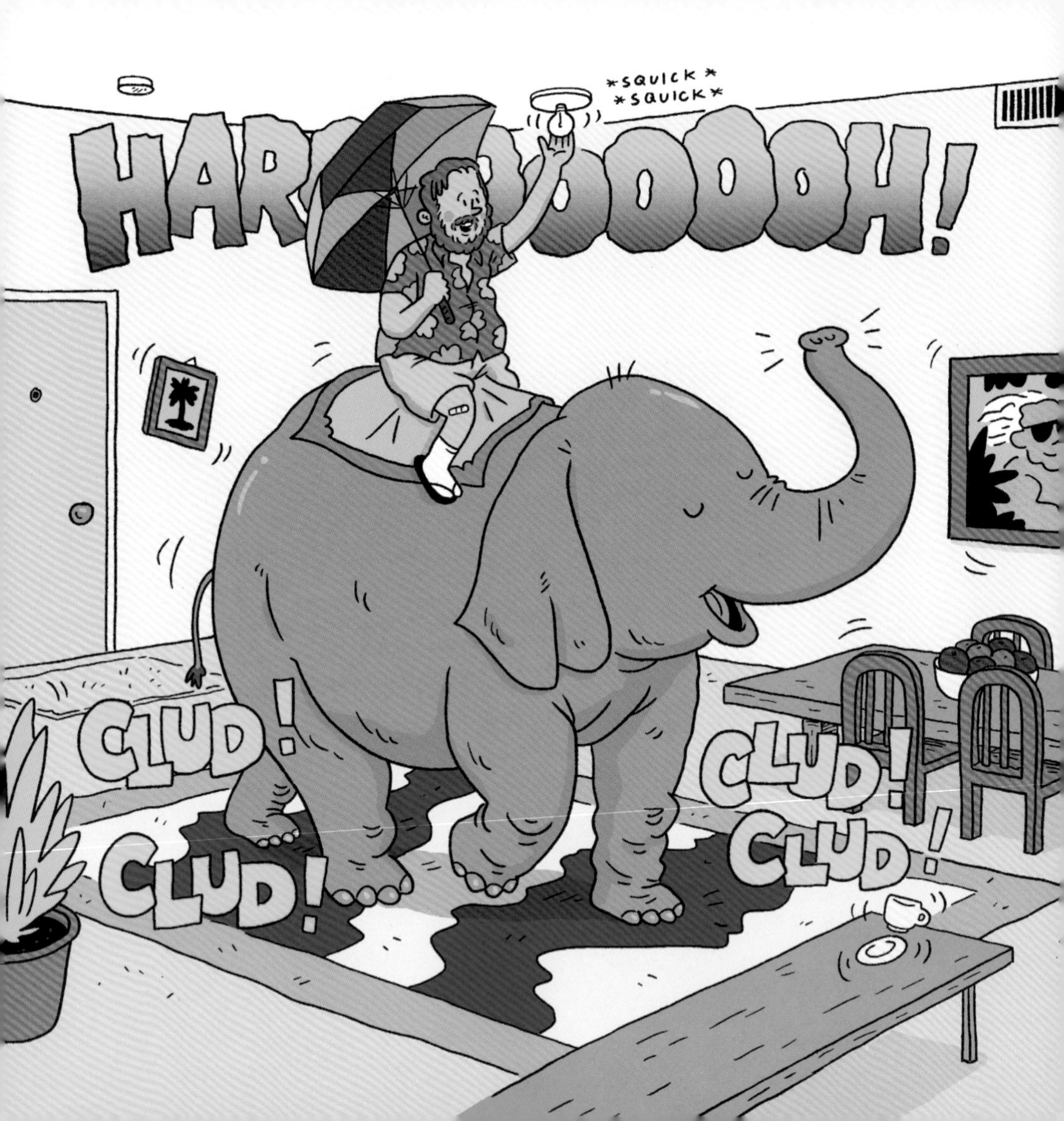
SQUICK
SQUICK
HAR OOOOOH!
CLUD!
CLUD!
CLUD!
CLUD!

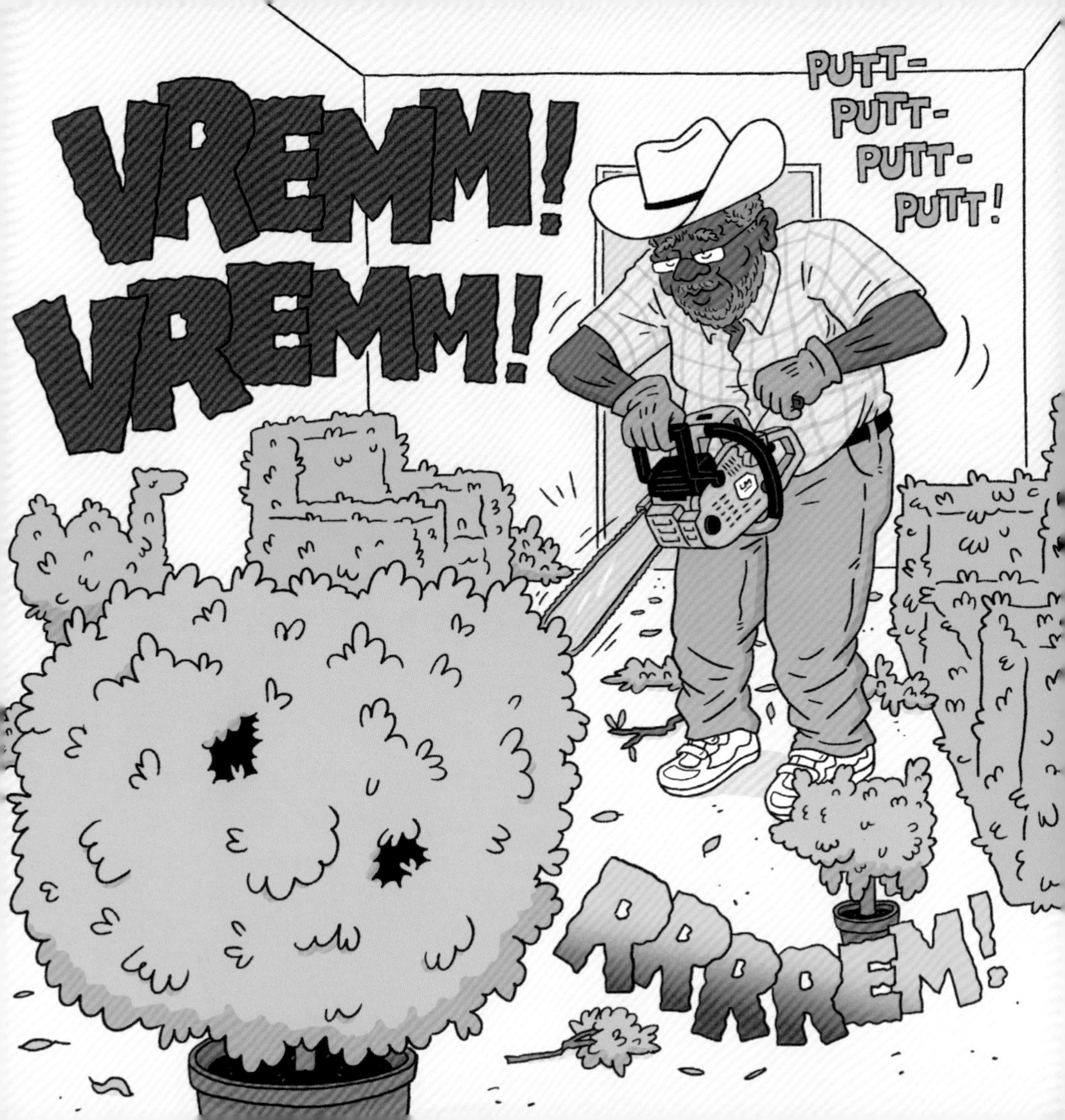
VREMM! VREMM!
PUTT-PUTT-PUTT-PUTT!
RRRREM!

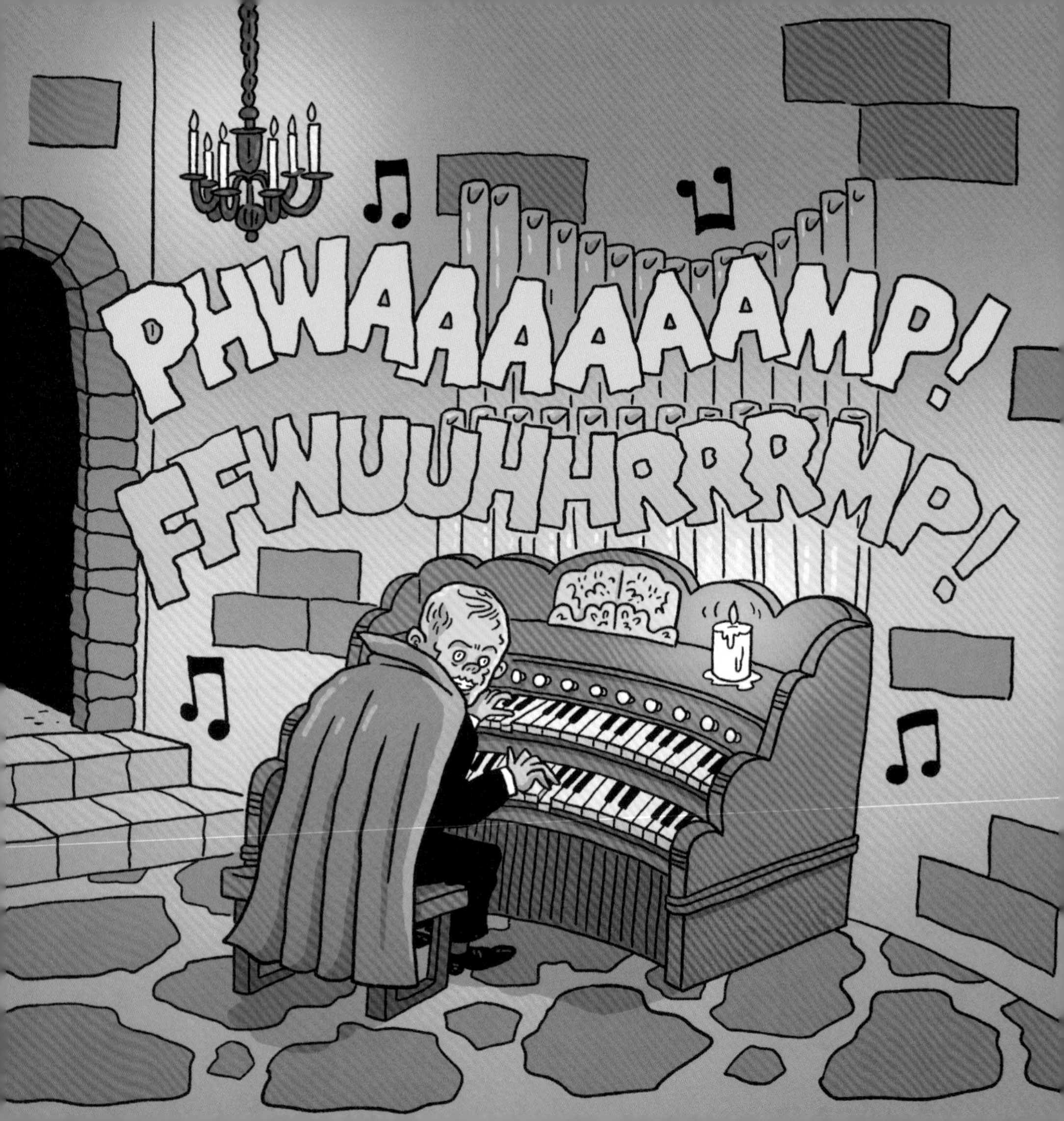
PHWAAAAAAAMP!
FFWUUHHRRRRMP!

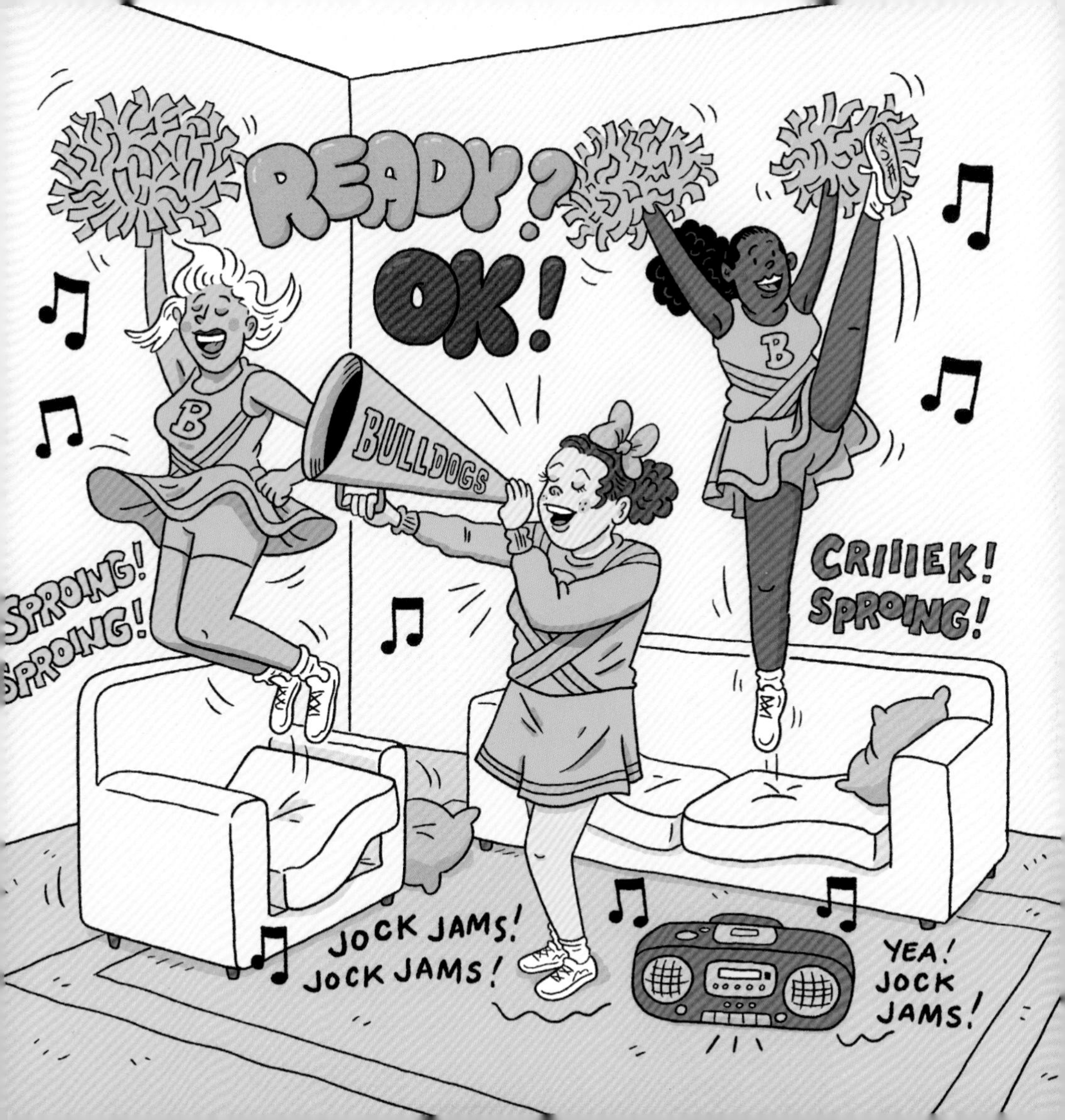
READY?
OK!
BULLDOGS
SPROING!
SPROING!
CRIIIEK!
SPROING!
JOCK JAMS!
JOCK JAMS!
YEA!
JOCK
JAMS!

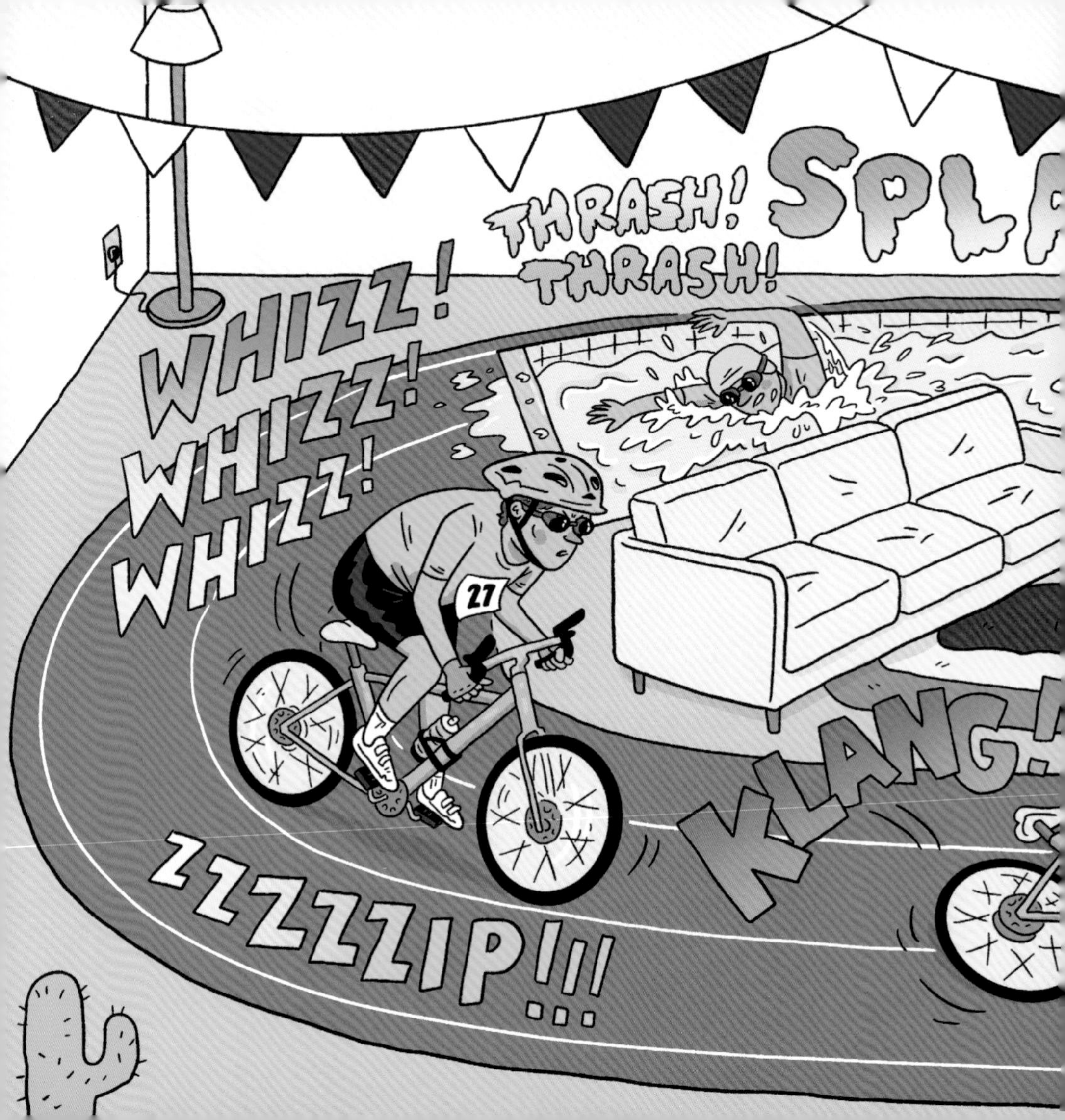
THRASH! THRASH!
WHIZZ! WHIZZ! WHIZZ!
27
KLANG!
ZZZZZZIP!!!

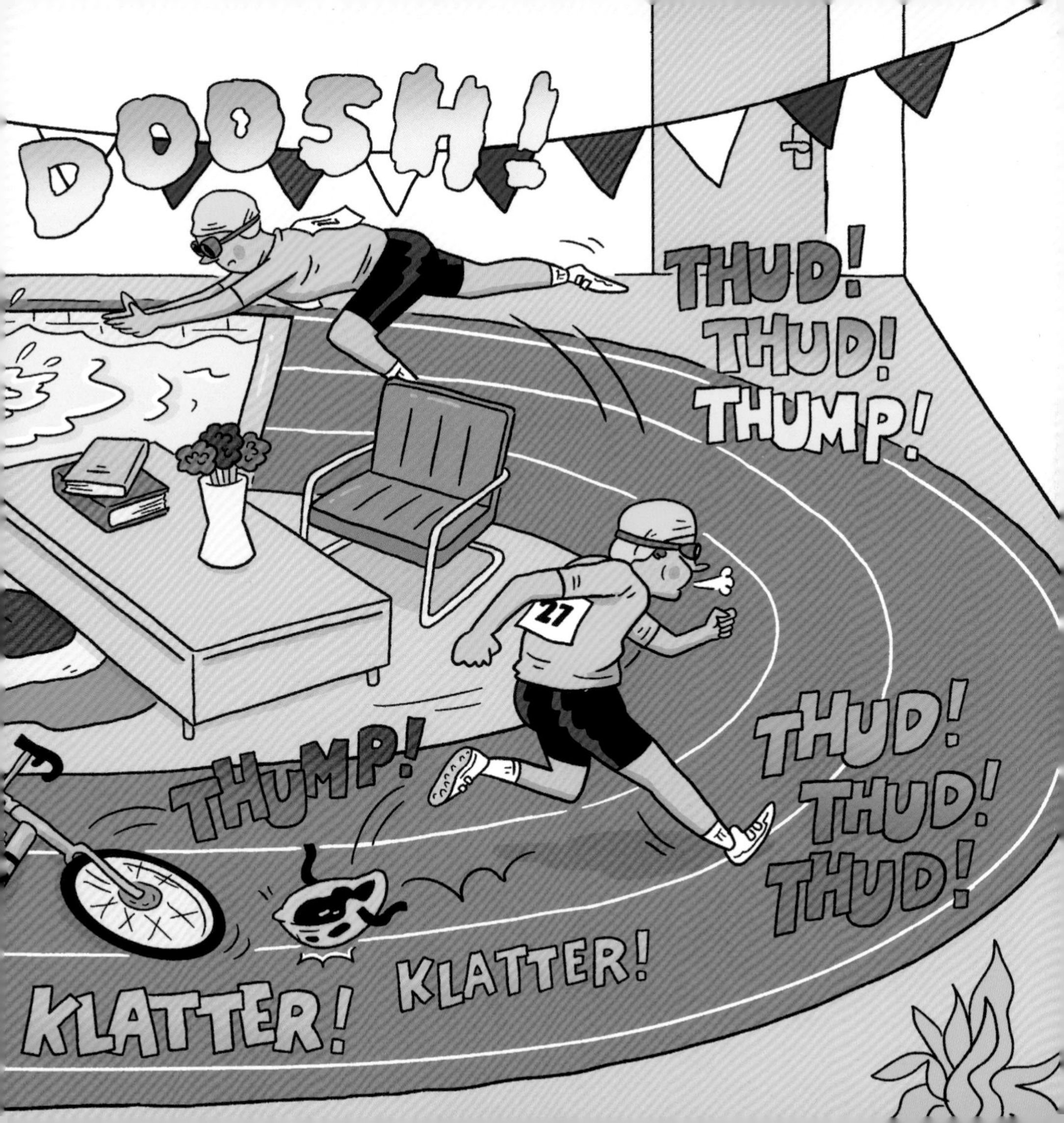
DOOSH!
THUD!
THUD!
THUMP!
THUMP!
THUD!
THUD!
THUD!
KLATTER!
KLATTER!

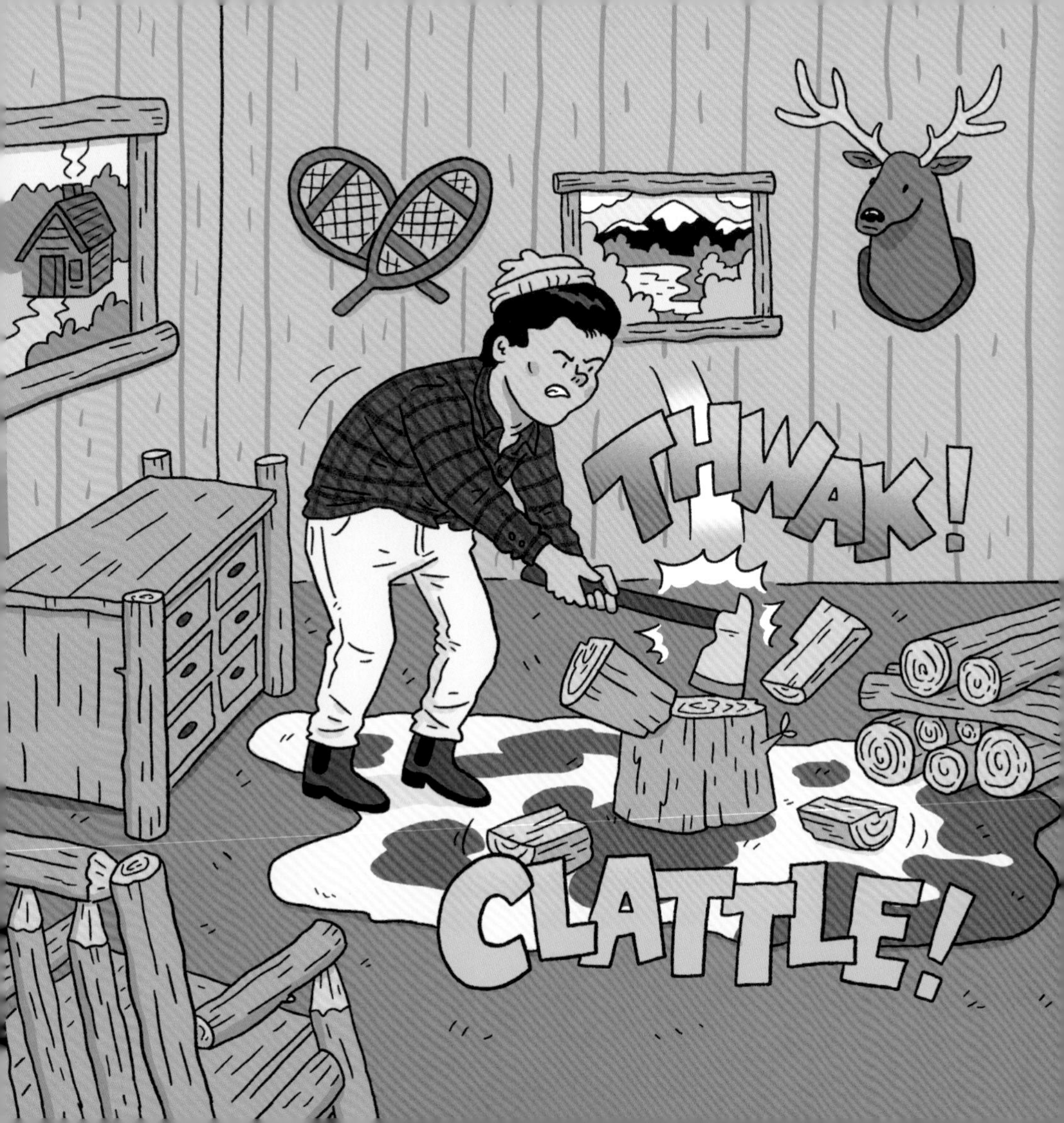
THWAK!
CLATTLE!

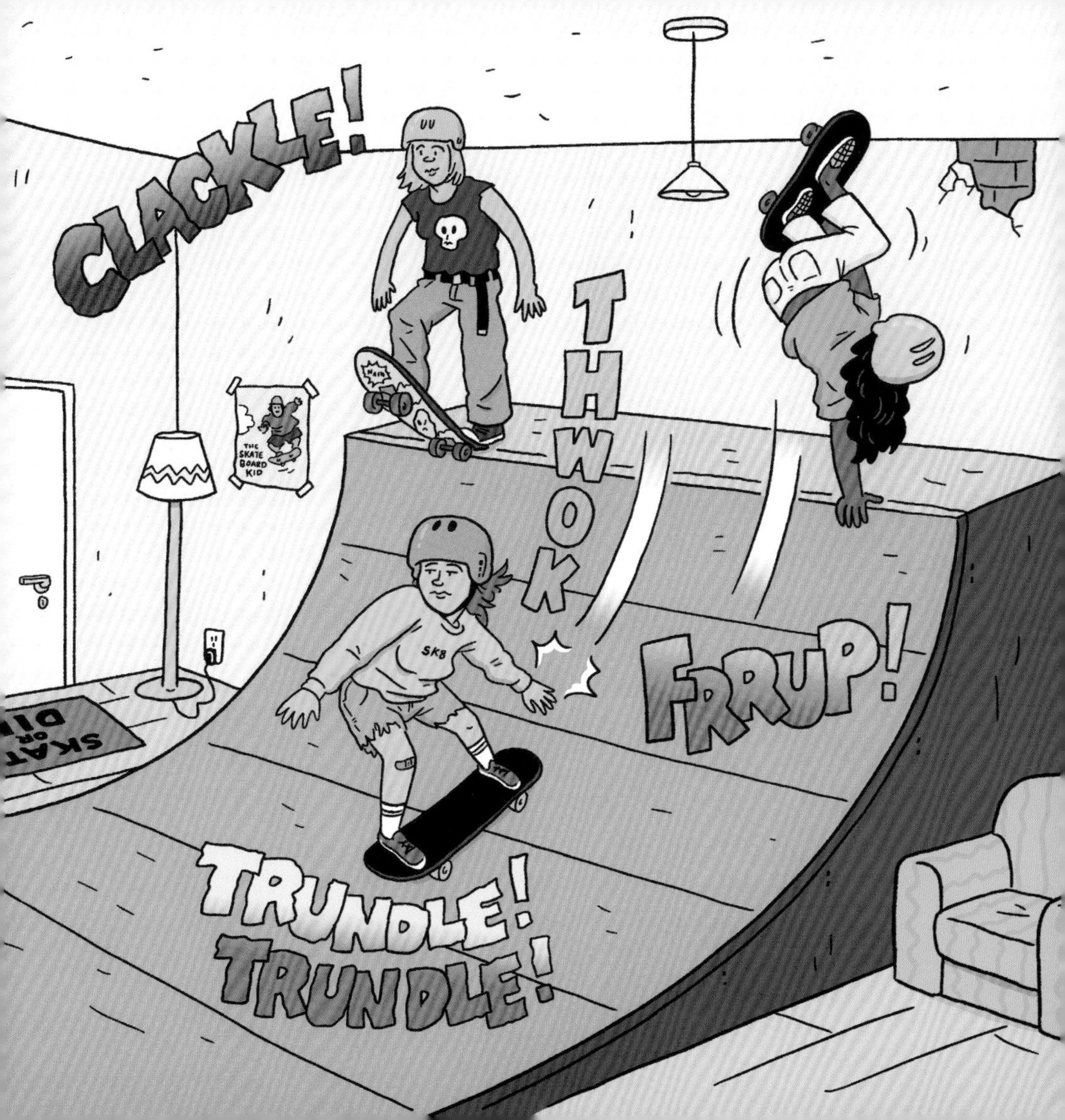
CLACKLE!
THE SKATE BOARD KID
THWOK
FRRUP!
SK8
TRUNDLE!
TRUNDLE!

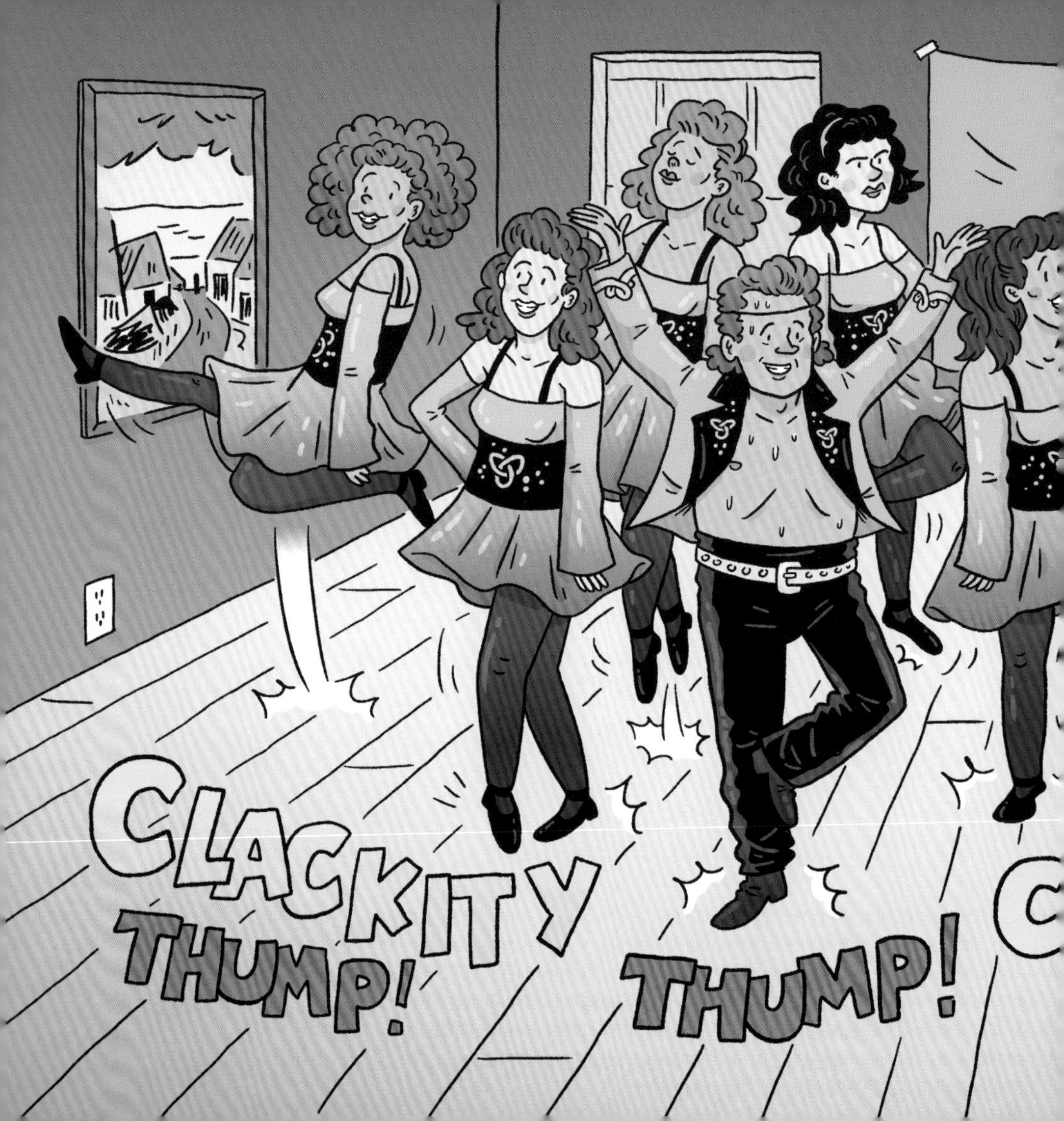
CLACKITY
THUMP!
THUMP!

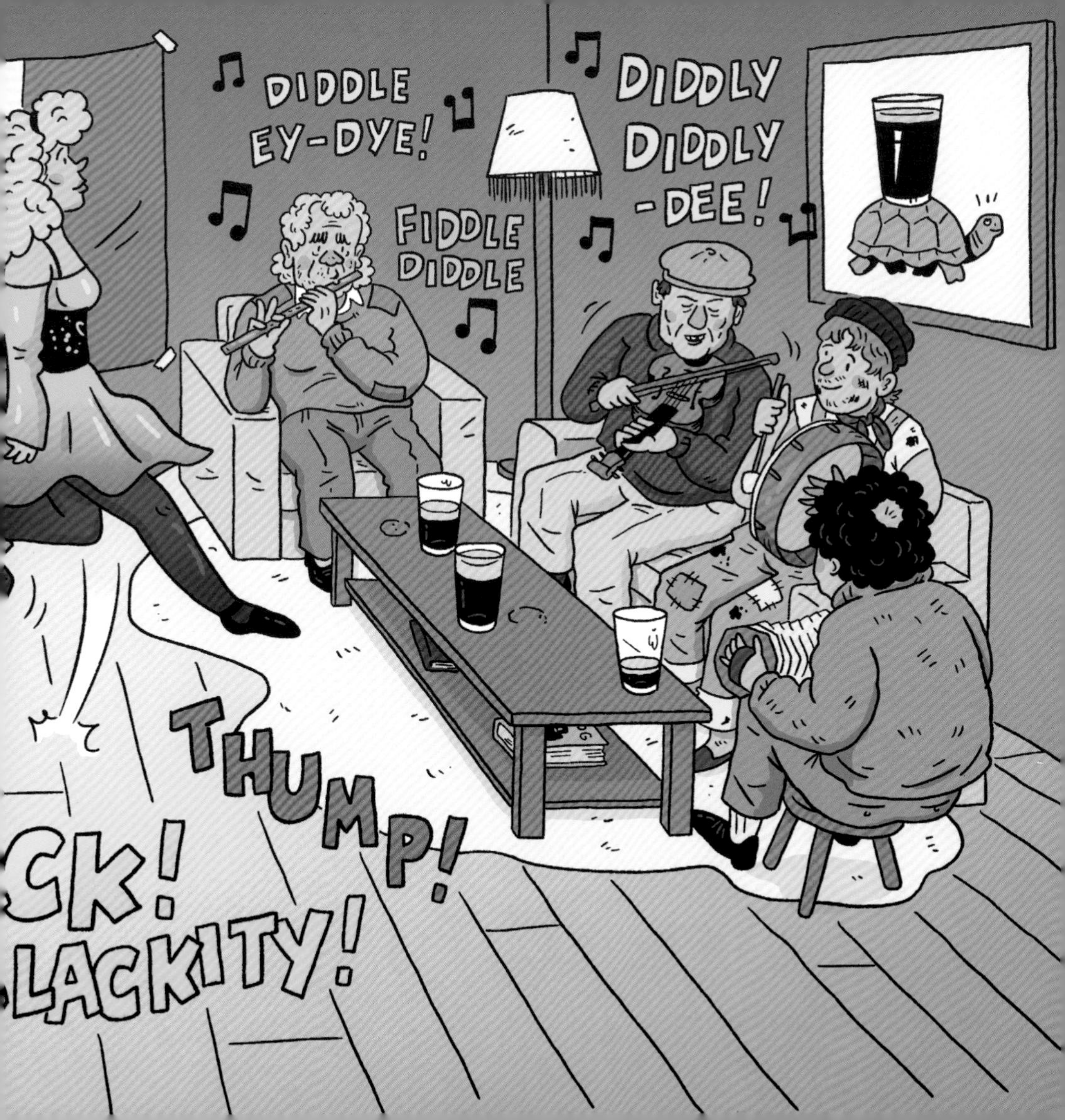
DIDDLE EY-DYE!
FIDDLE DIDDLE
DIDDLY DIDDLY -DEE!
THUMP!
CK!
LACKITY!

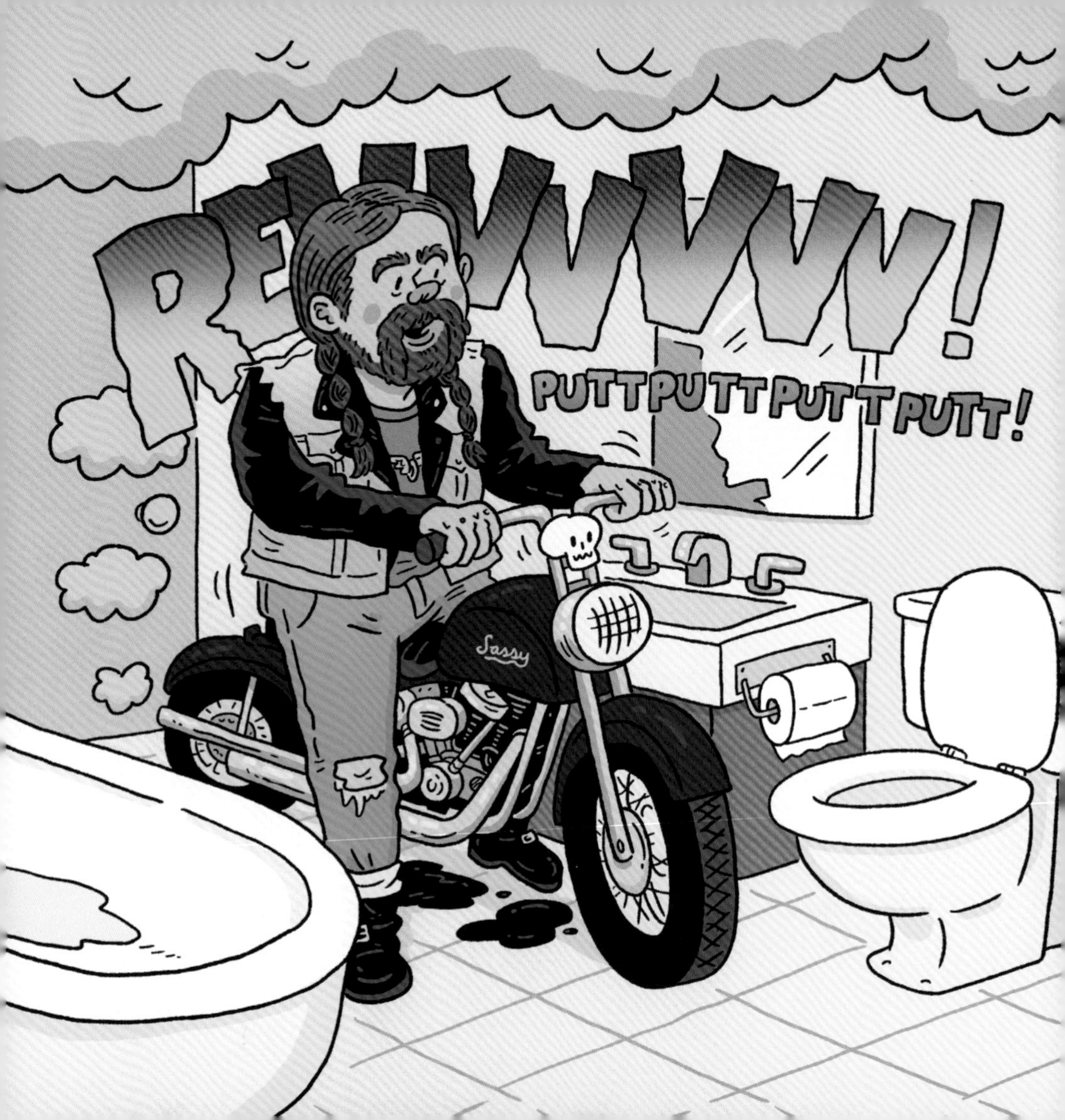
PUTT PUTT PUTT PUTT!
Sassy

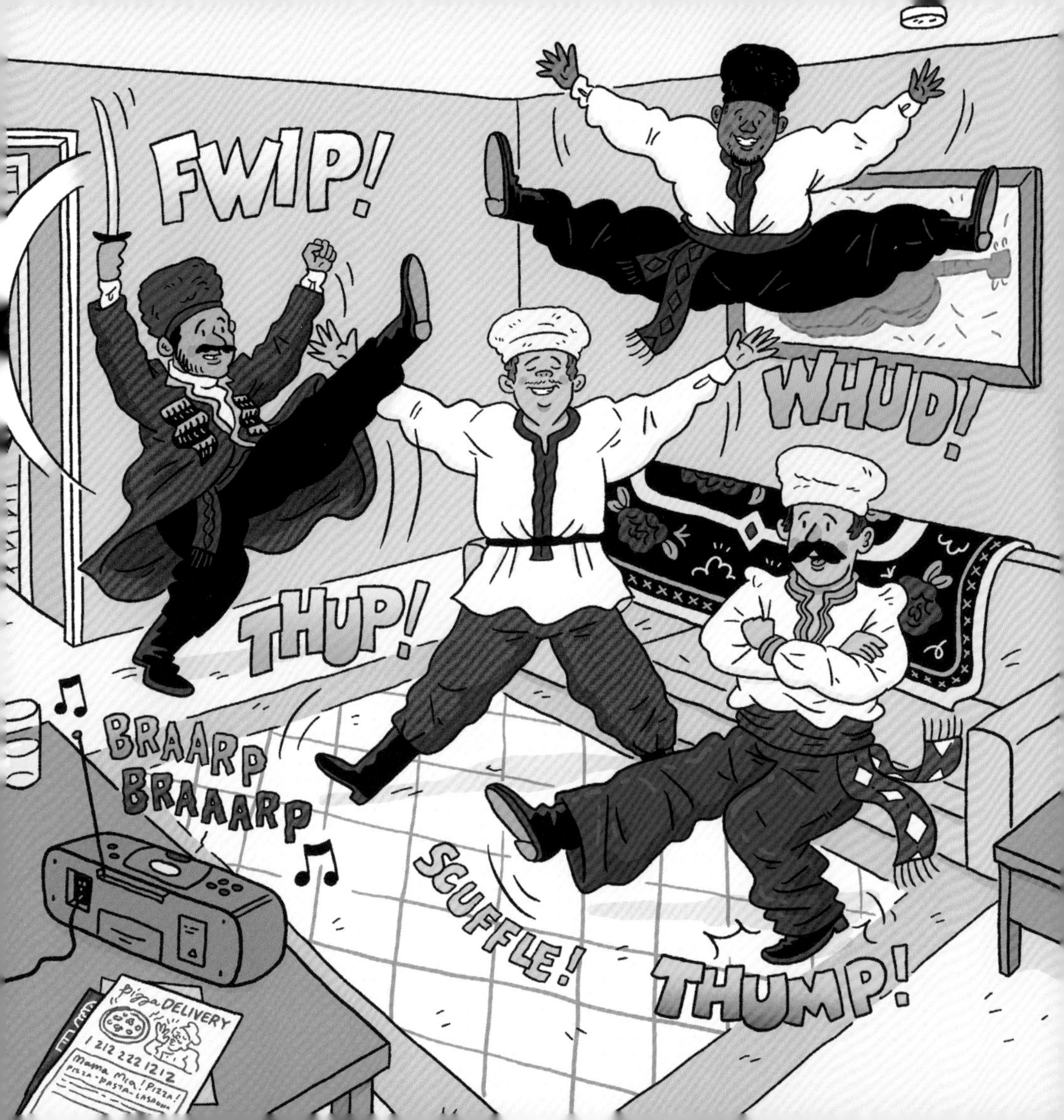
FWIP!
WHUD!
THUP!
BRAARP
BRAAARP
SCUFFLE!
THUMP!
Pizza DELIVERY
1 212 222 1212
Mama Mia! Pizza!
PIZZA-PASTA-LASAGNA

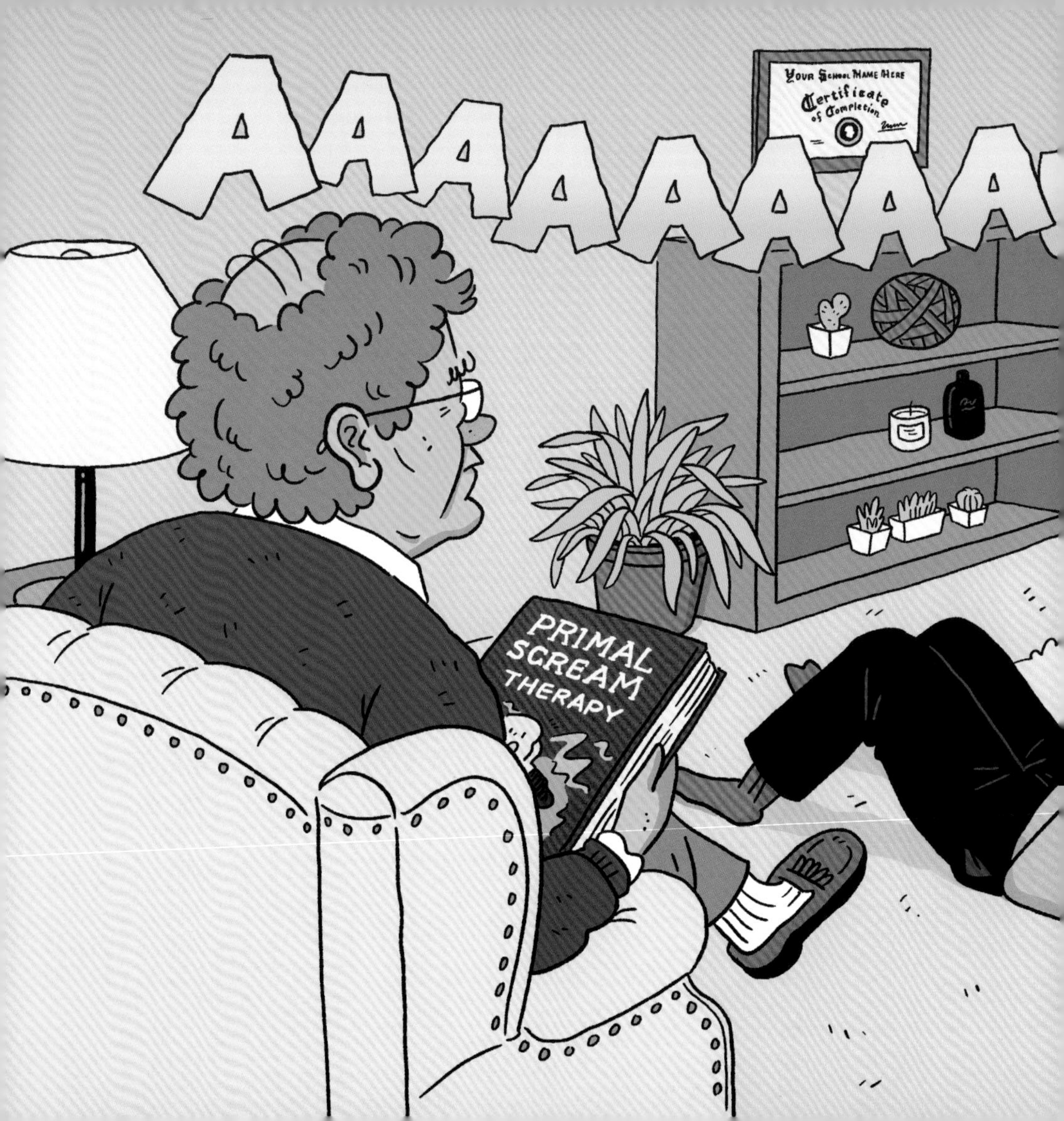
AAAAAAAAA
YOUR SCHOOL NAME HERE
Certificate of Completion
PRIMAL SCREAM THERAPY

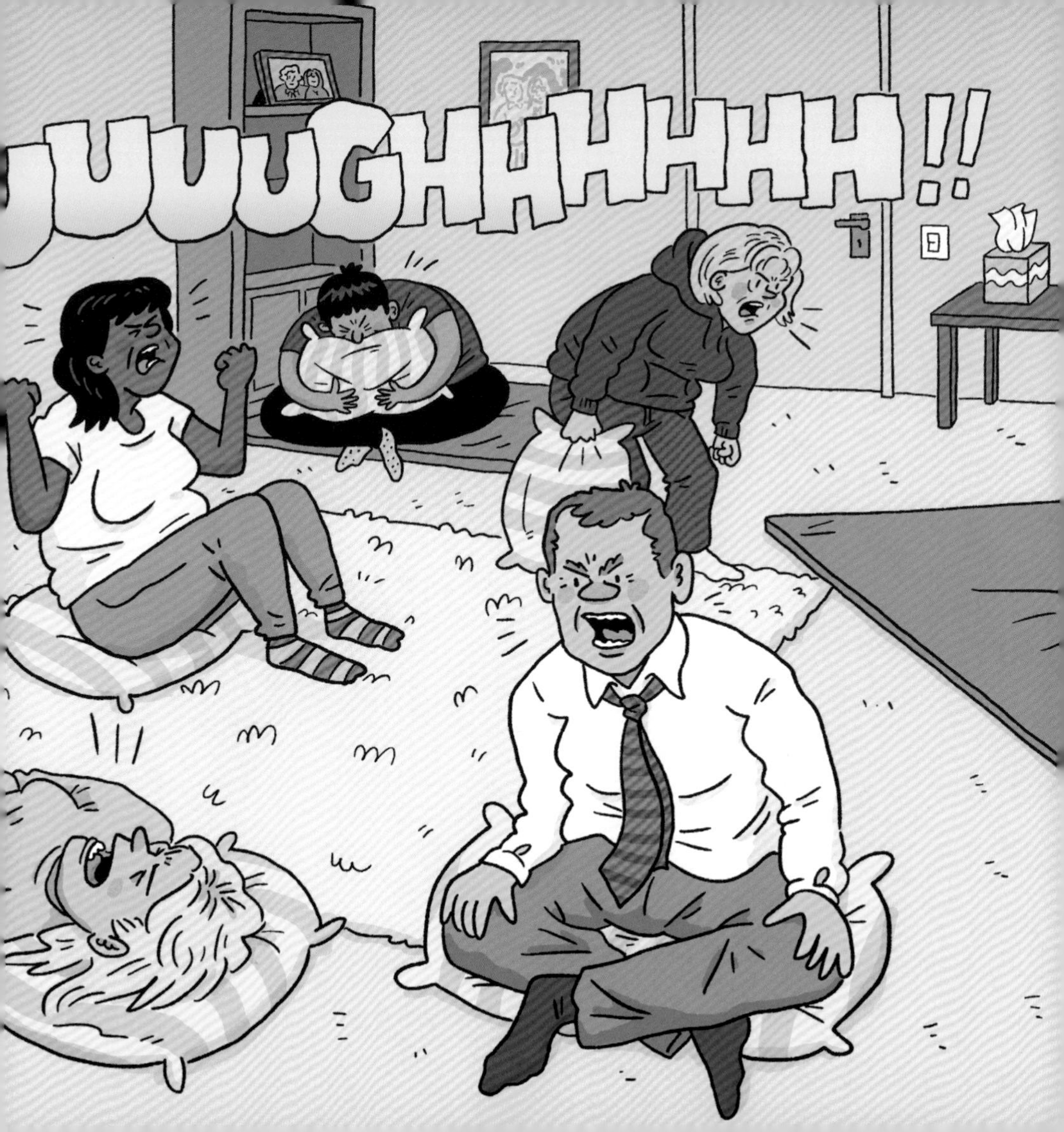
UUUUGHHHHHHH!!

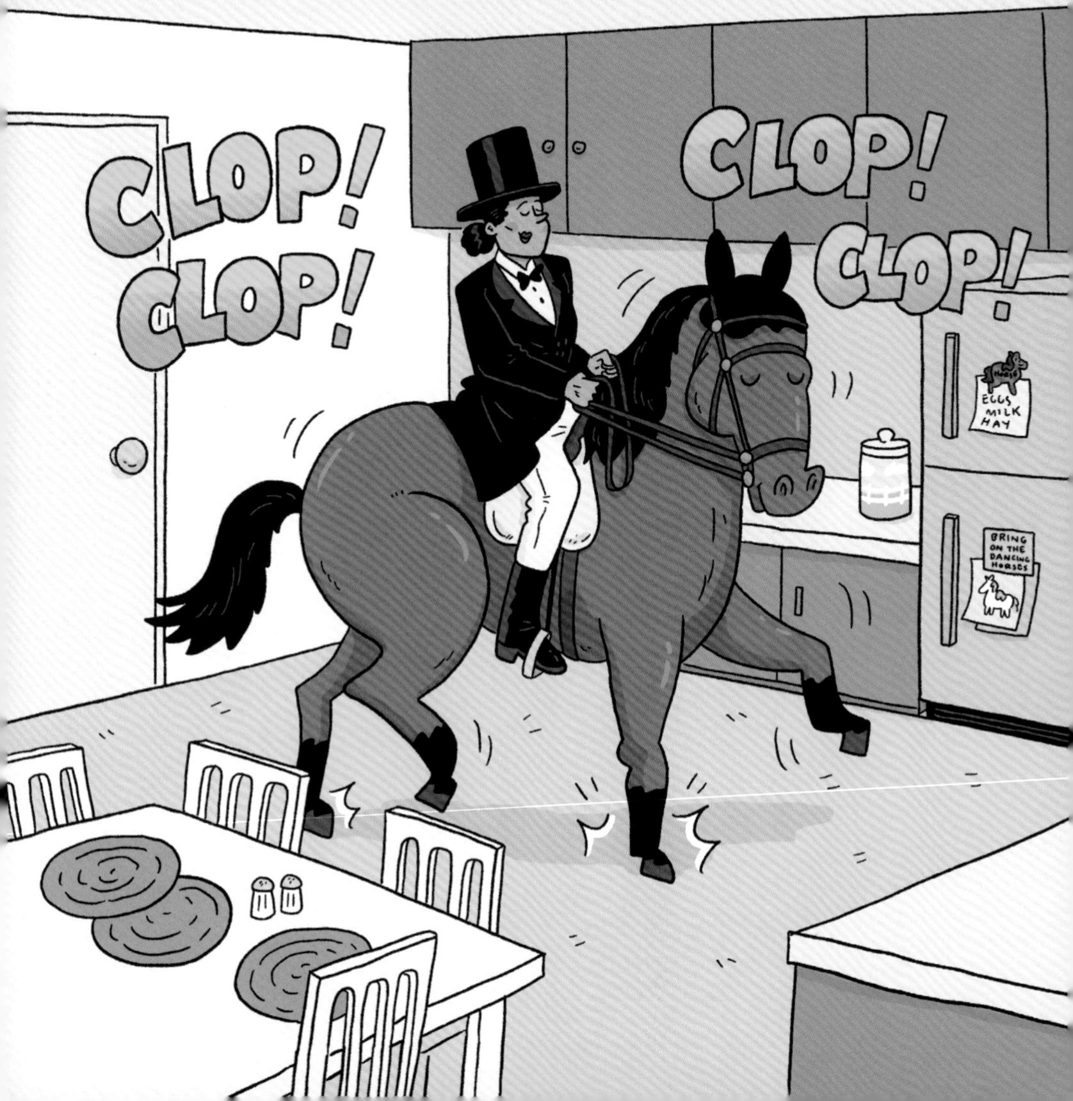
CLOP!
CLOP!
CLOP!
CLOP!
HORSE
EGGS
MILK
HAY
BRING ON THE DANCING HORSES

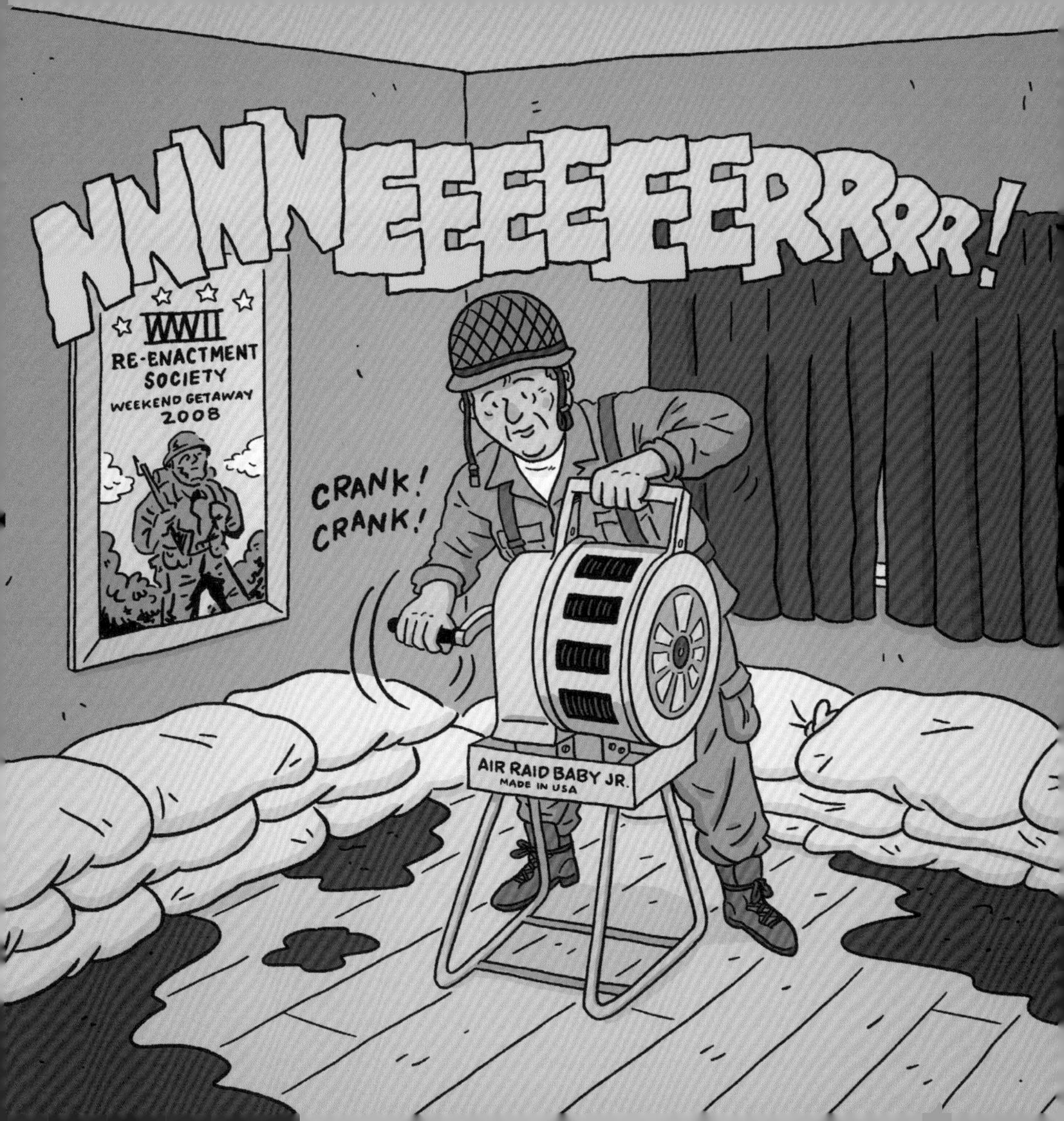

NNNNEEEEEERRRRR!
WWII
RE-ENACTMENT
SOCIETY
WEEKEND GETAWAY
2008
CRANK!
CRANK!
AIR RAID BABY JR.
MADE IN USA

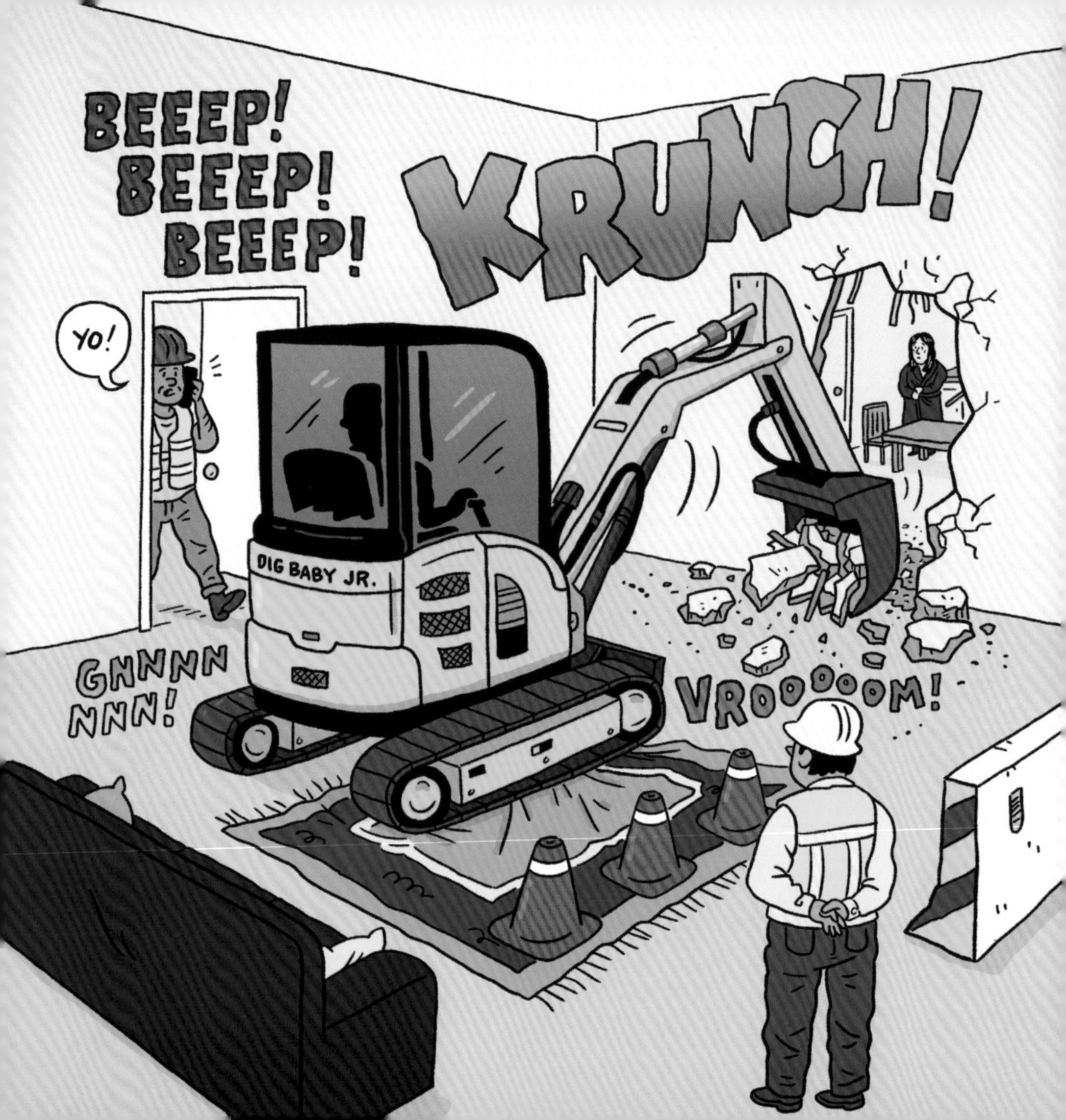
BEEEP! BEEEP! BEEEP!
KRUNCH!
YO!
DIG BABY JR.
GNNNN NNN!
VROOOOOOM!

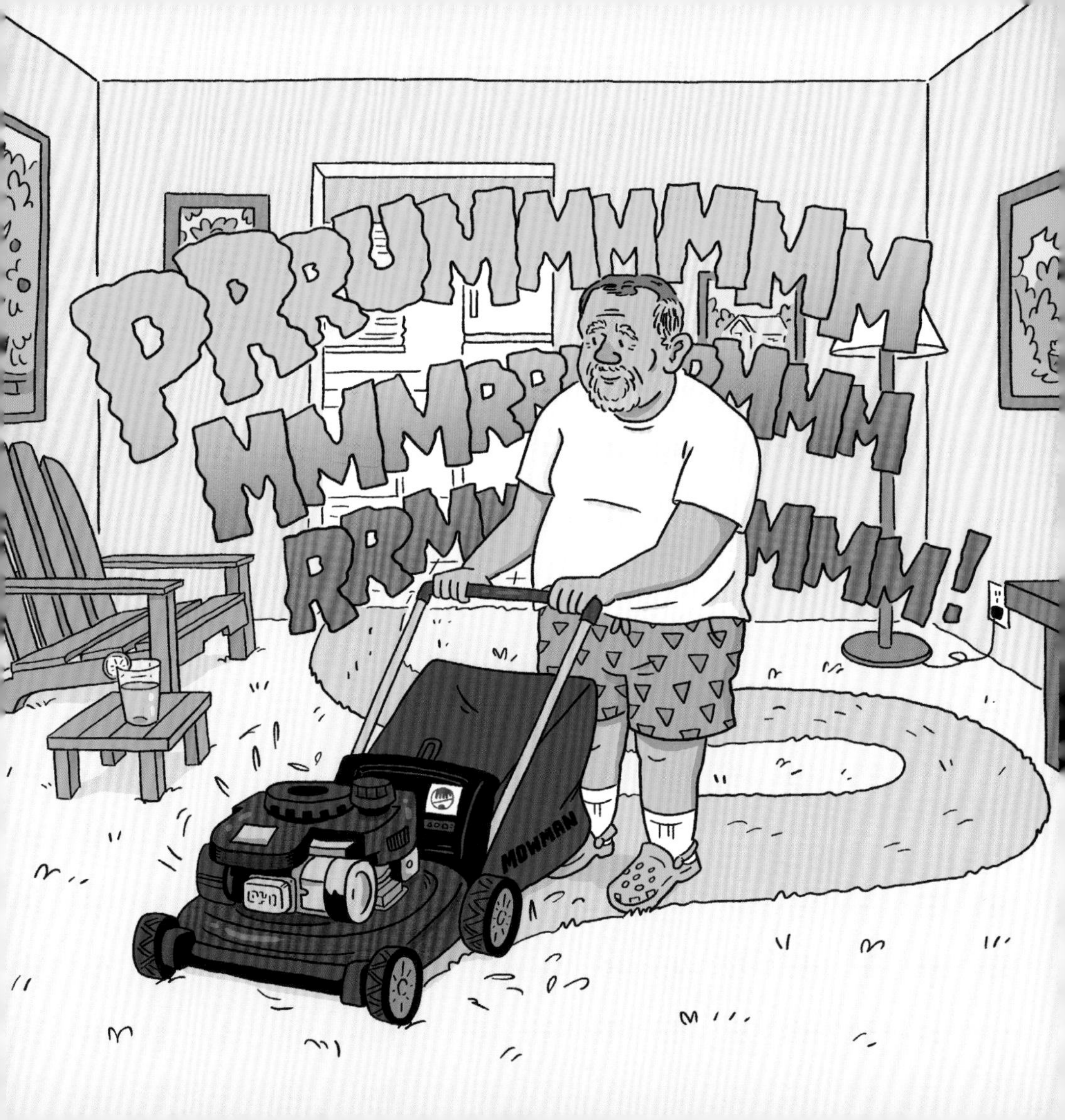
PRRUMMMMMMM
MOWMAN

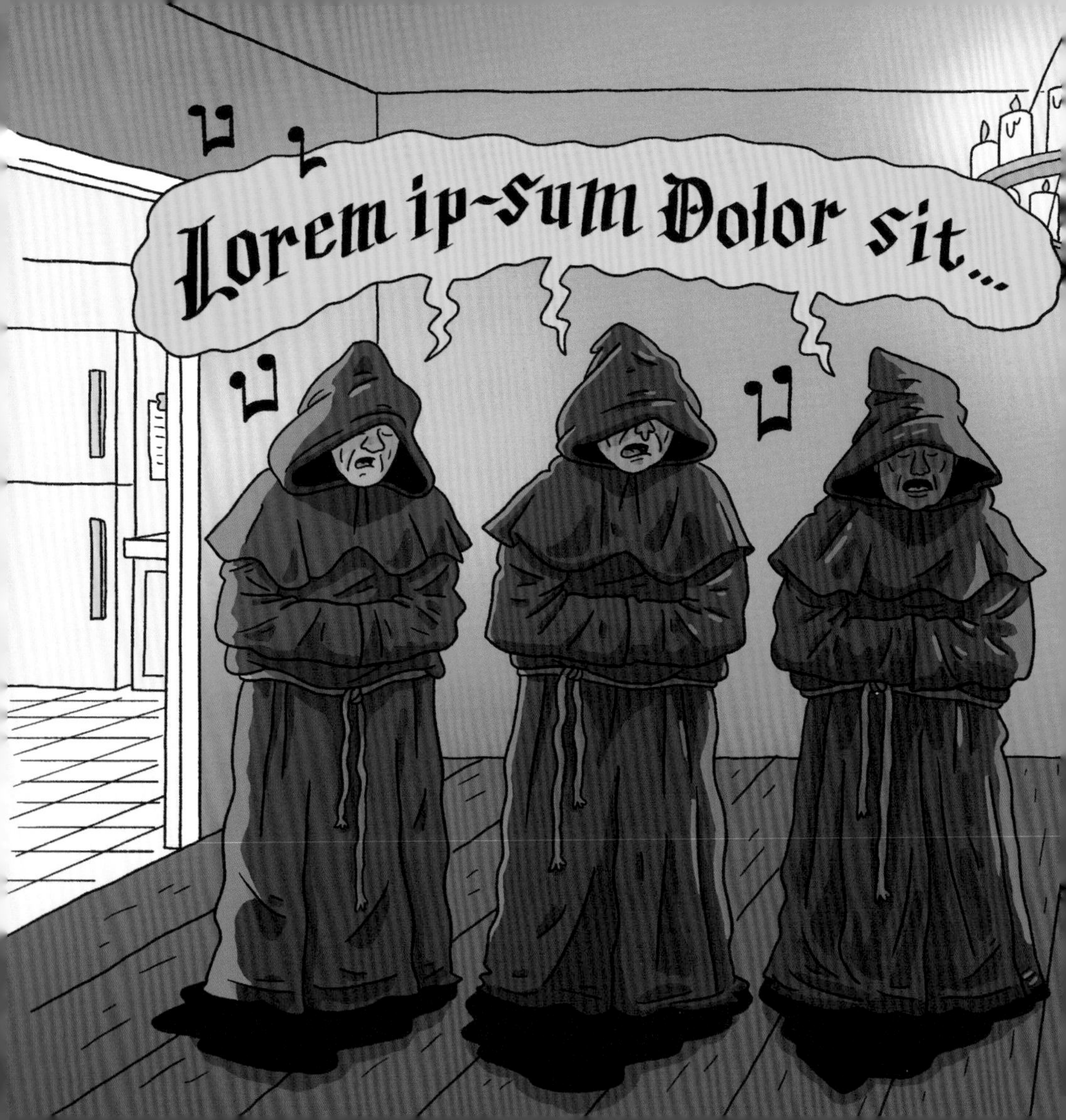
Lorem ip-sum Dolor sit...

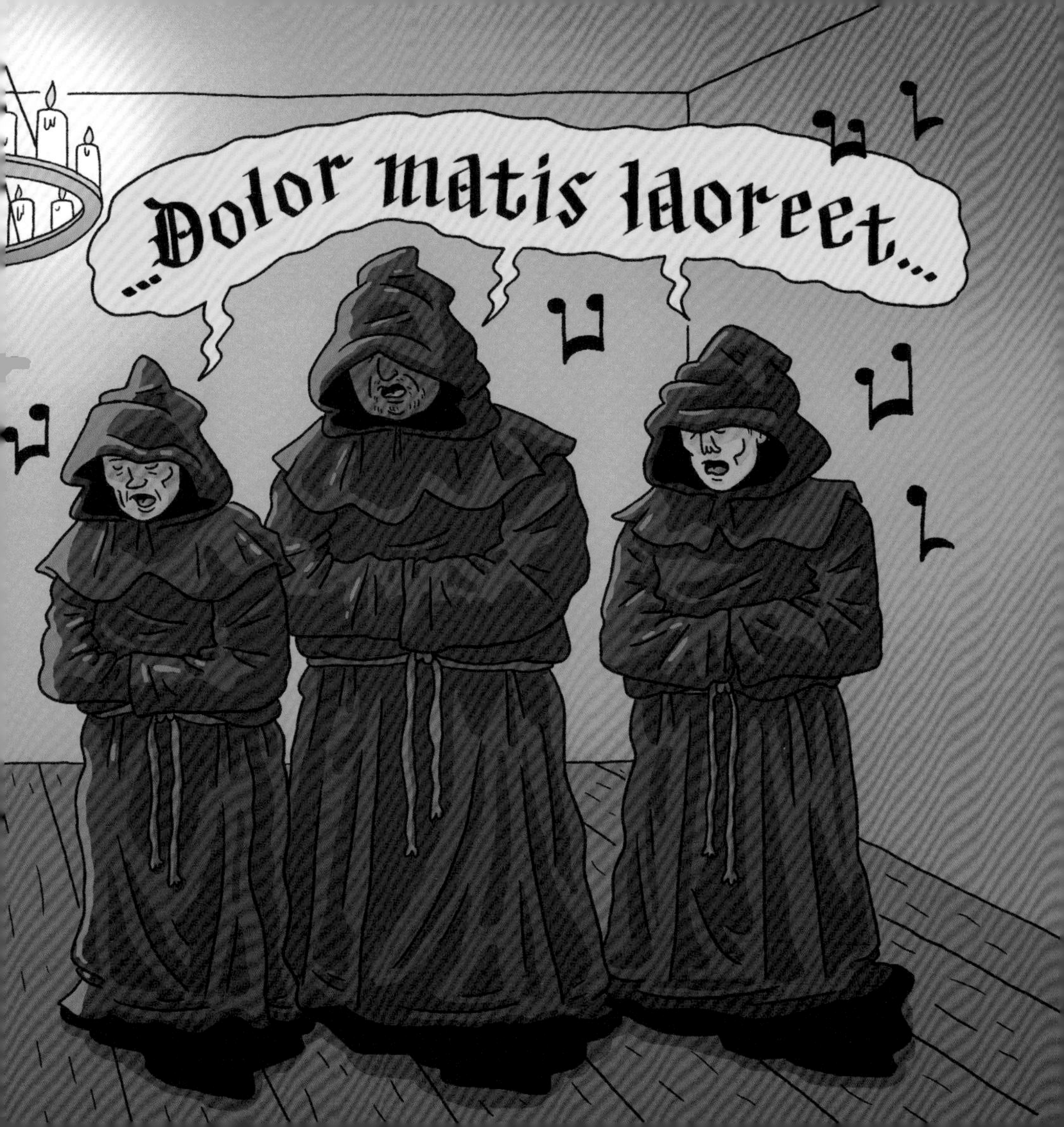
...Dolor matis laoreet...

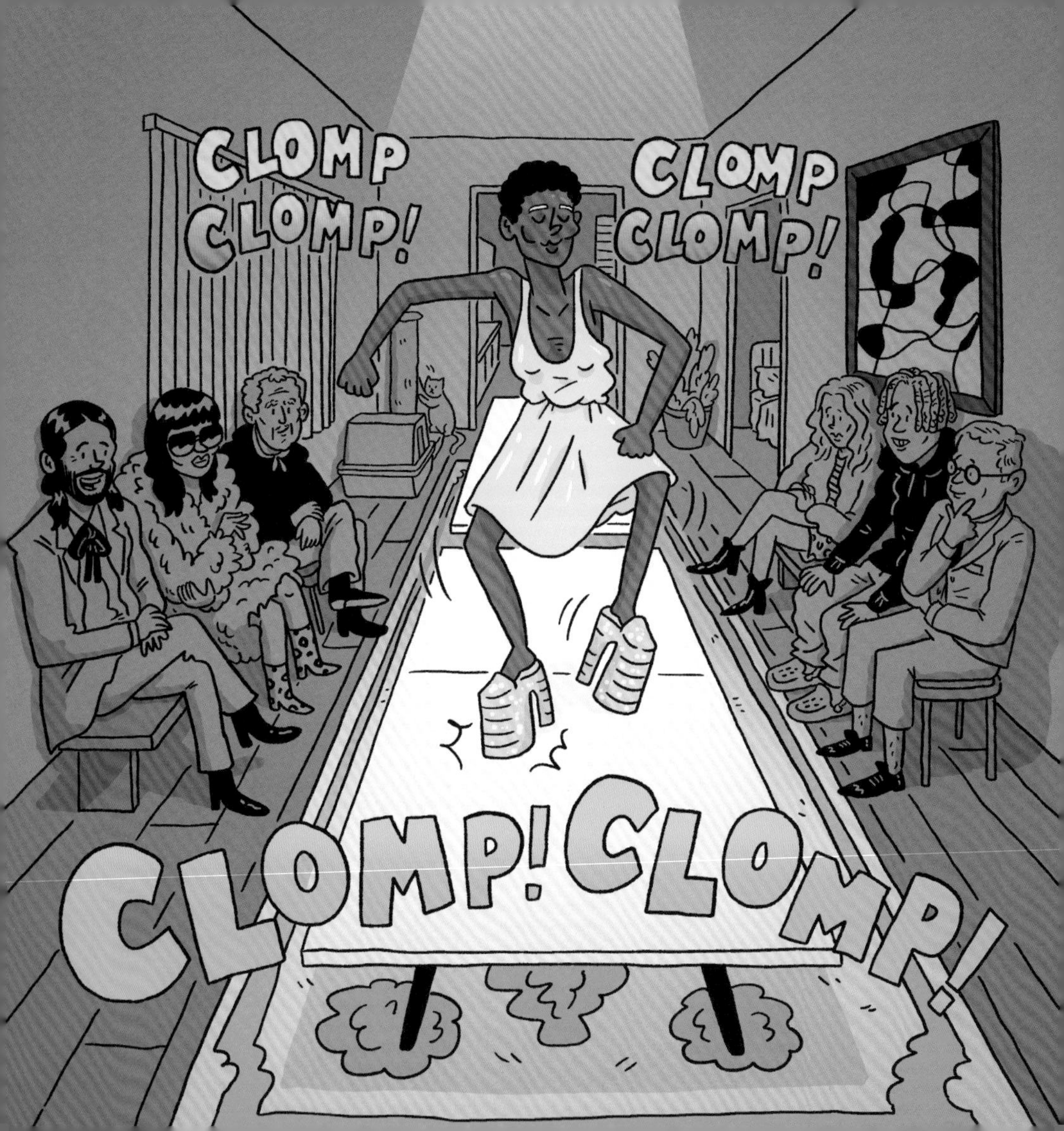
CLOMP CLOMP!
CLOMP CLOMP!
CLOMP! CLOMP!

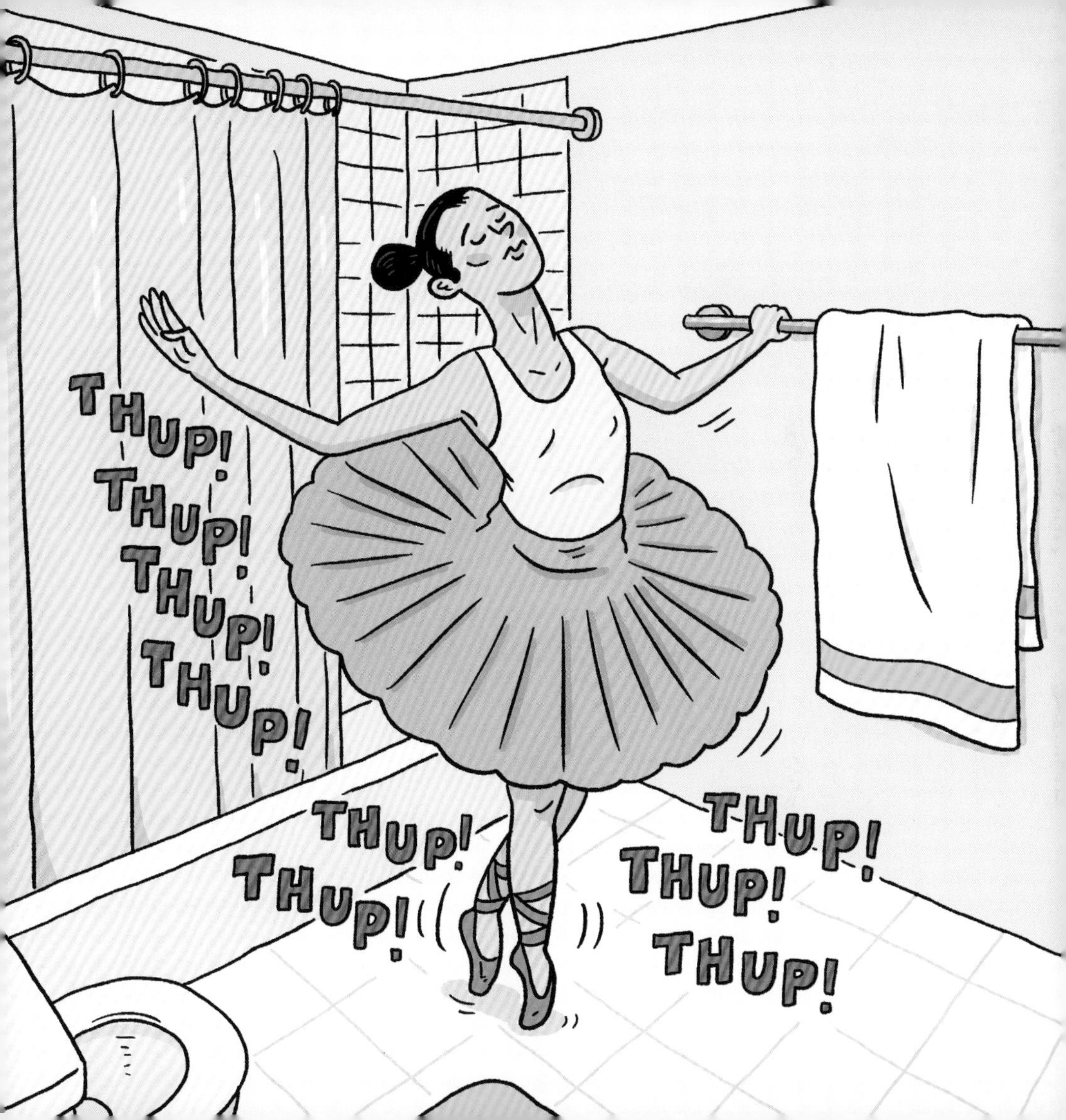
THUP!
THUP!
THUP!
THUP!
THUP!
THUP!
THUP!
THUP!
THUP!

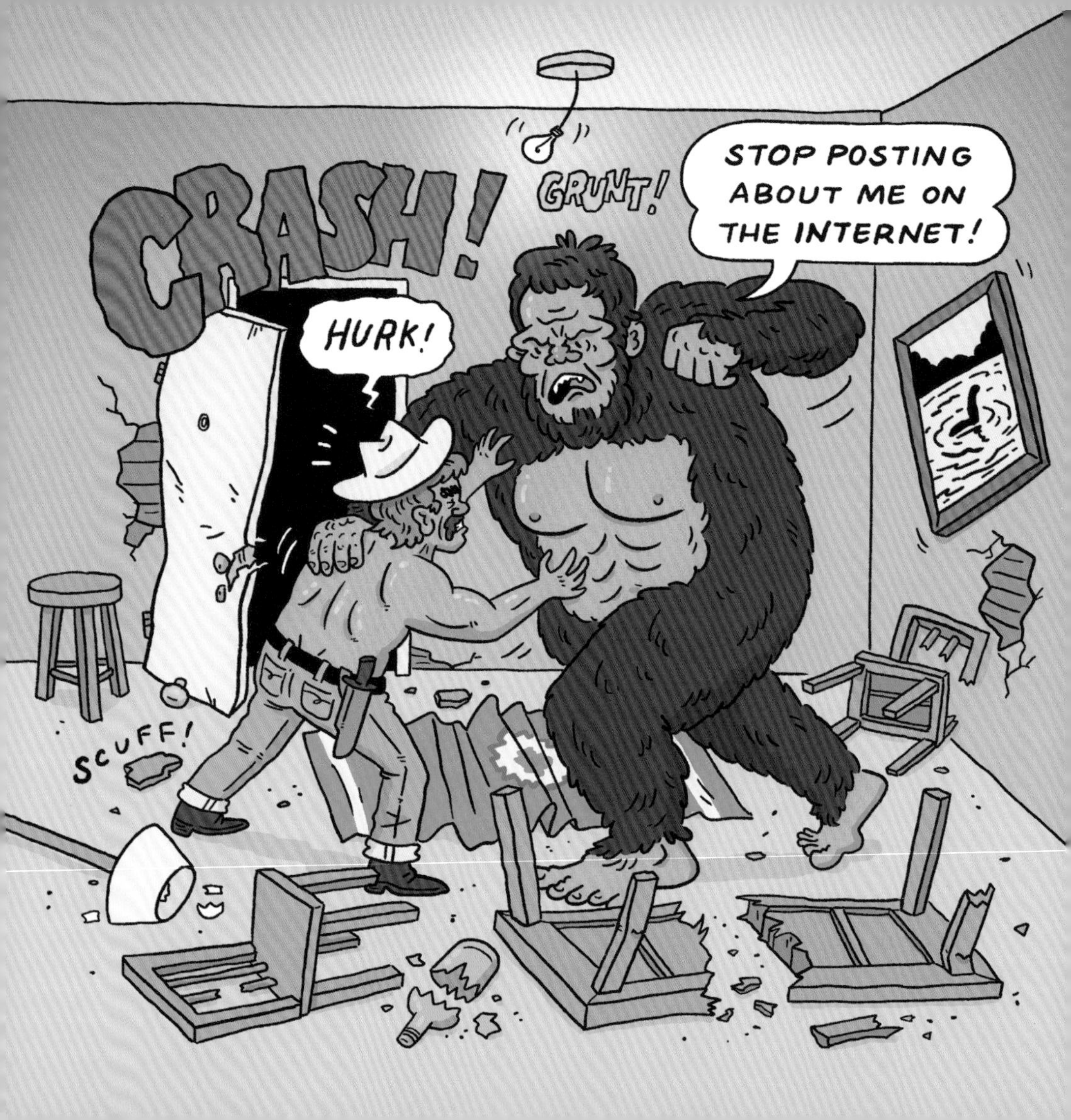
CRASH!
GRUNT!
STOP POSTING ABOUT ME ON THE INTERNET!
HURK!
SCUFF!

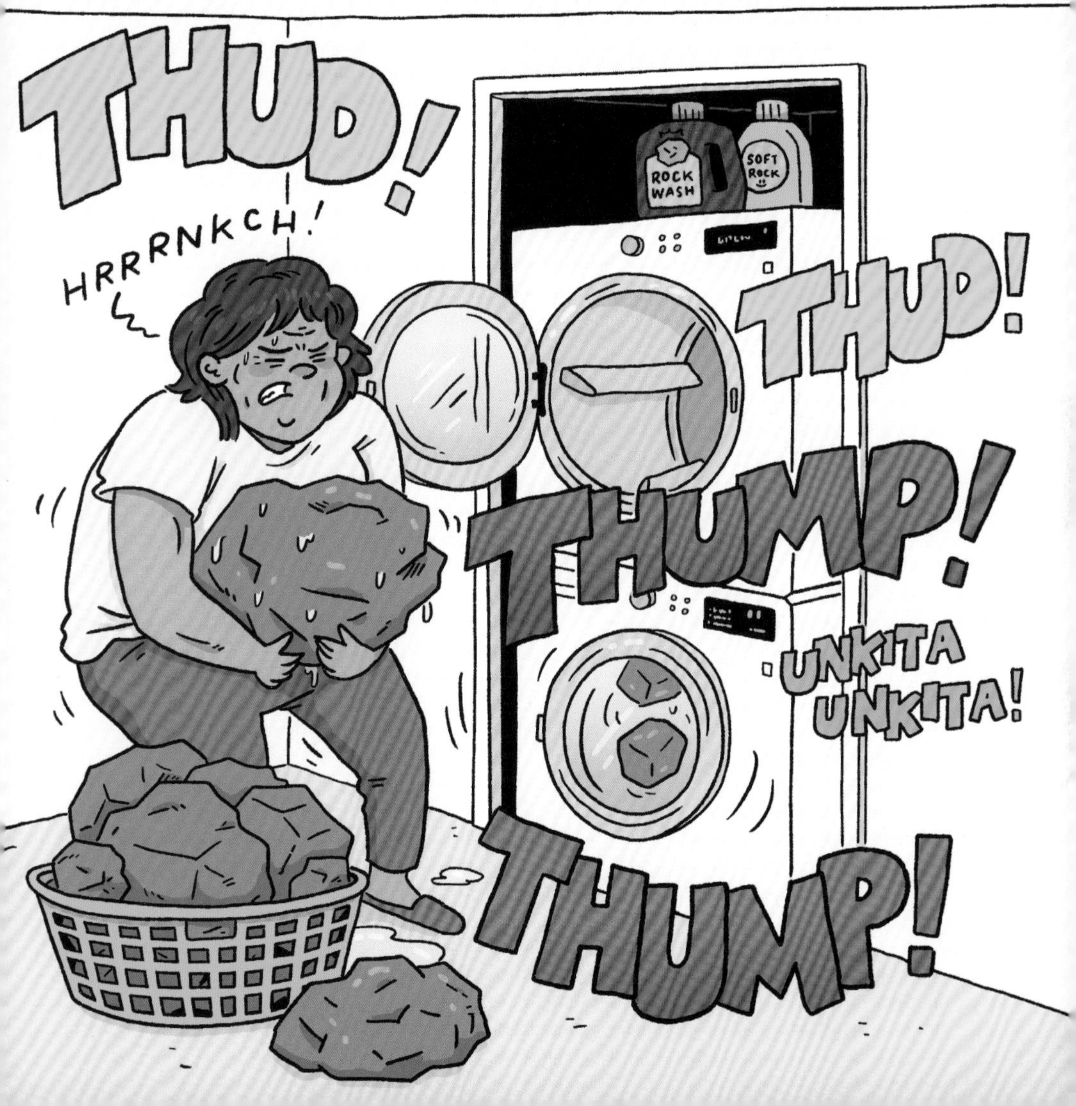
THUD!
HRRRNKCH!
THUD!
THUMP!
UNKITA UNKITA!
THUMP!
ROCK WASH
SOFT ROCK

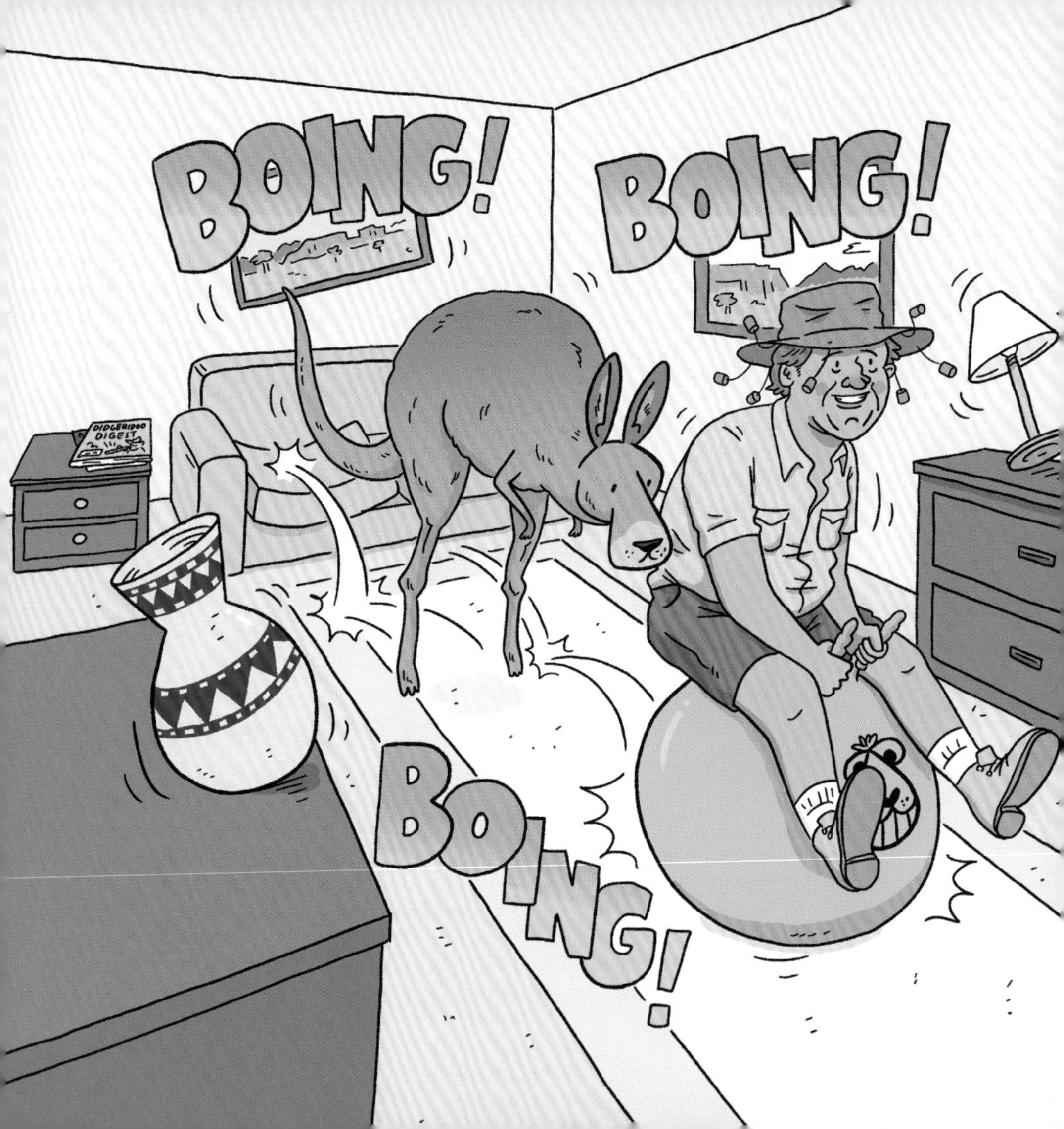
BOING!
BOING!
DIDGERIDOO DIGEST
BOING!

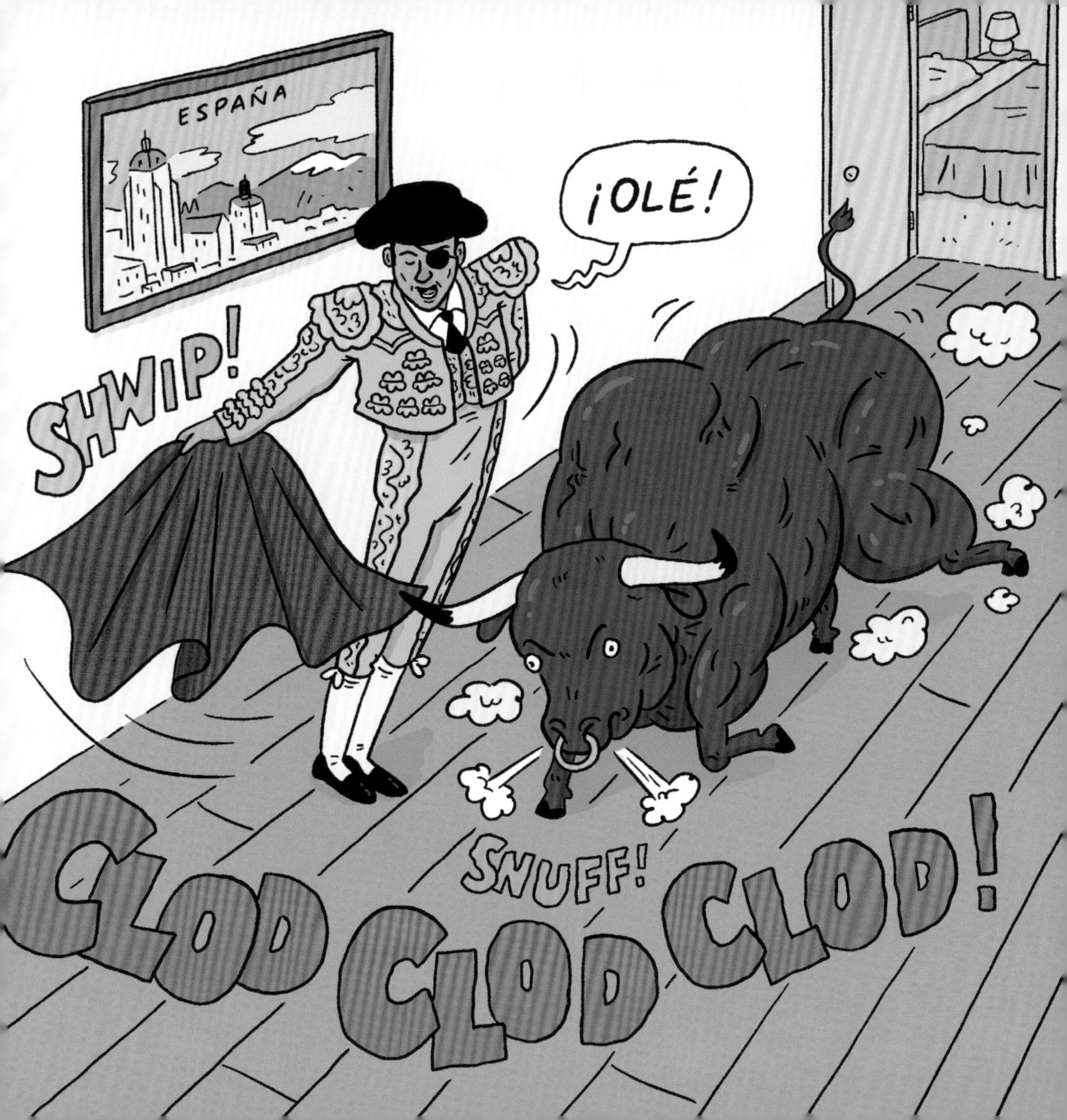
ESPAÑA
¡OLÉ!
SHWIP!
SNUFF!
CLOD CLOD CLOD!

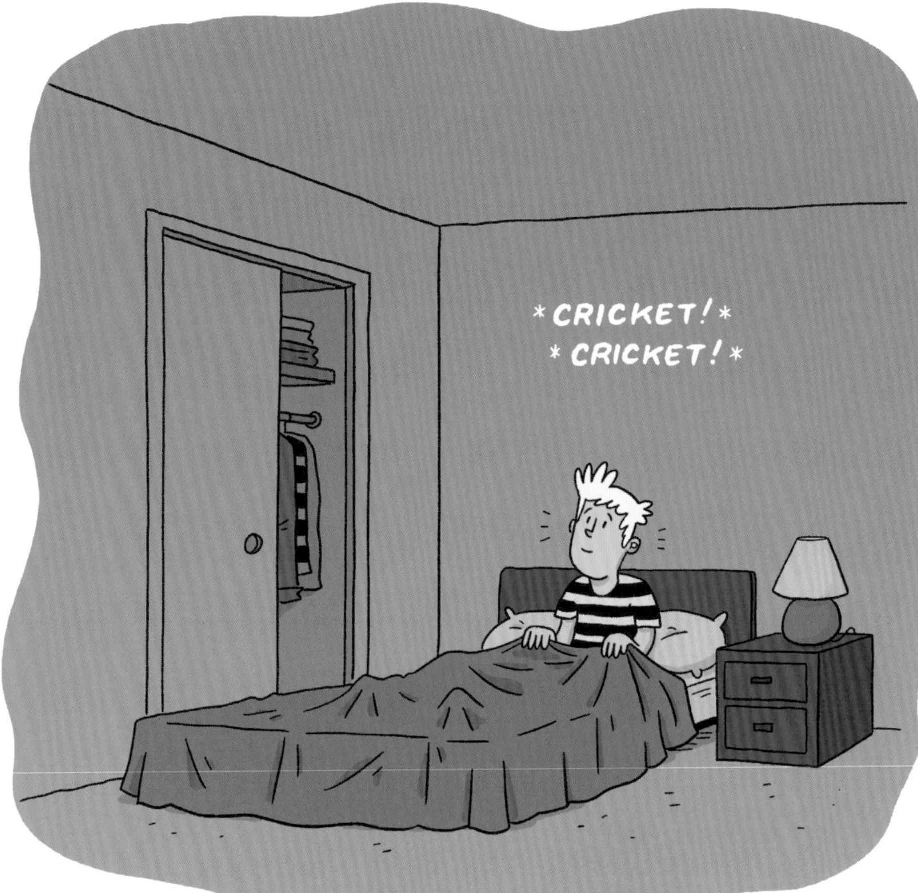
CRICKET!
CRICKET!

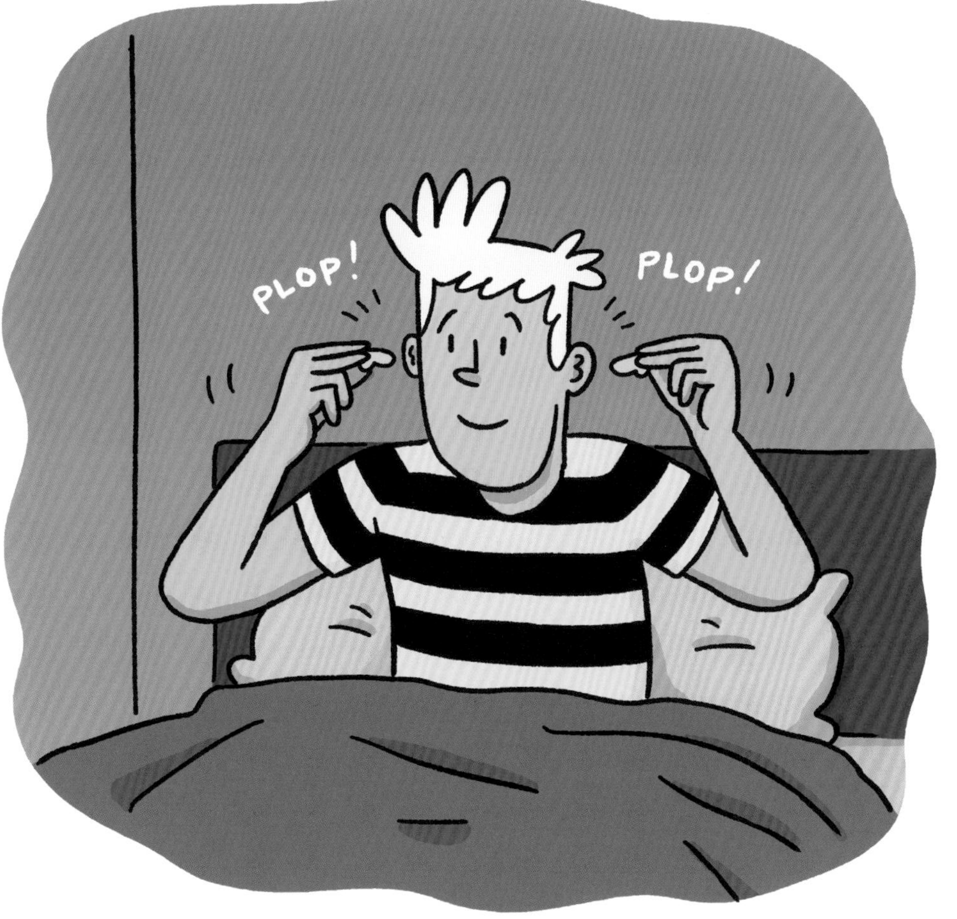
PLOP!
PLOP!

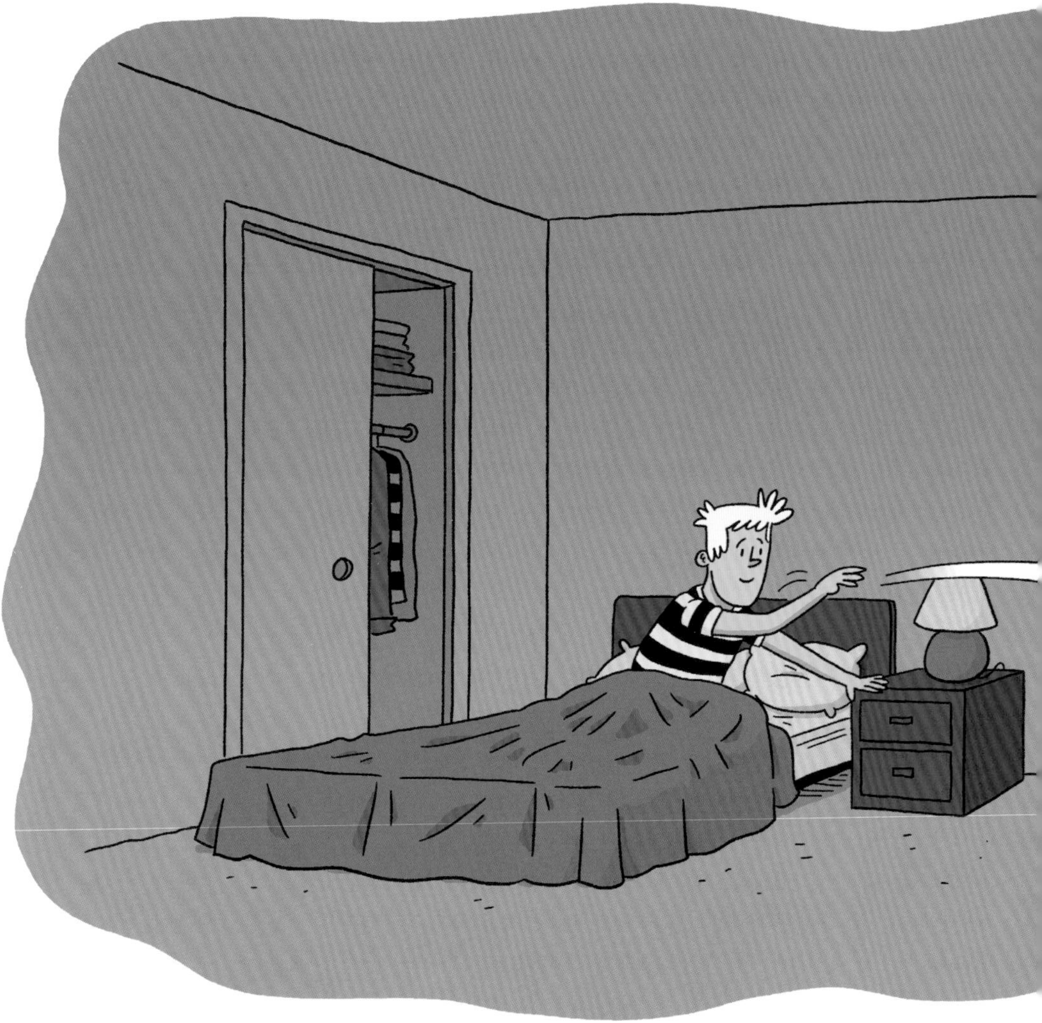

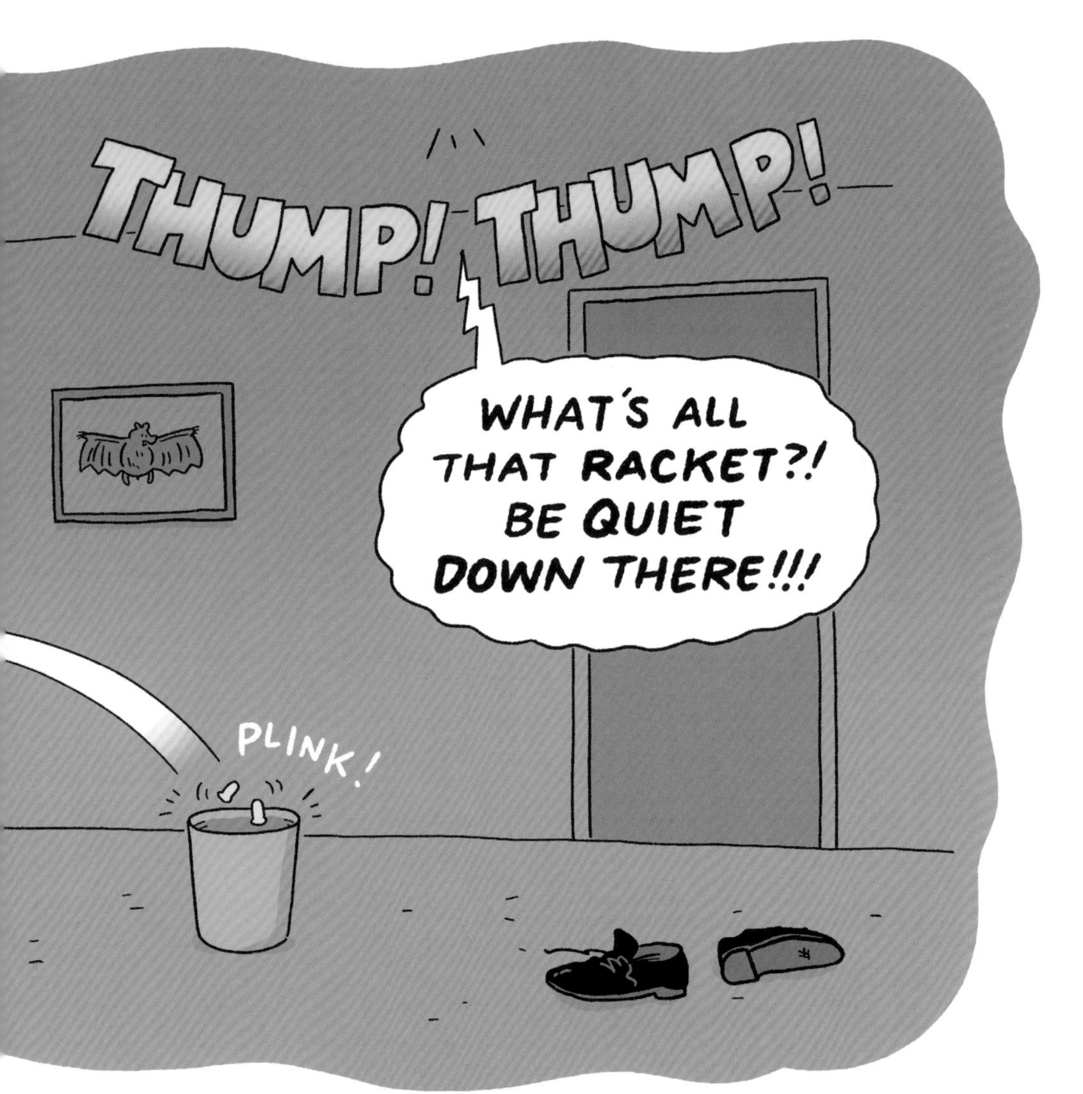
THUMP! THUMP!
WHAT'S ALL THAT RACKET?! BE QUIET DOWN THERE!!!
PLINK!

Luke McGarry is a British-born cartoonist, animator, and musician, currently residing in Los Angeles's noisiest apartment building.

He has been furnished with several illustration awards from the National Cartoonists Society and one cease and desist letter from the city of Santa Monica.

Luke's clients include the *New Yorker*, *Playboy*, and *MAD* magazine.

CRASH

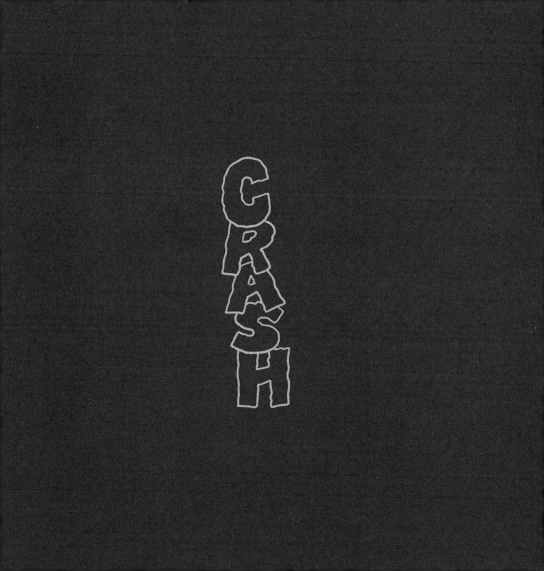

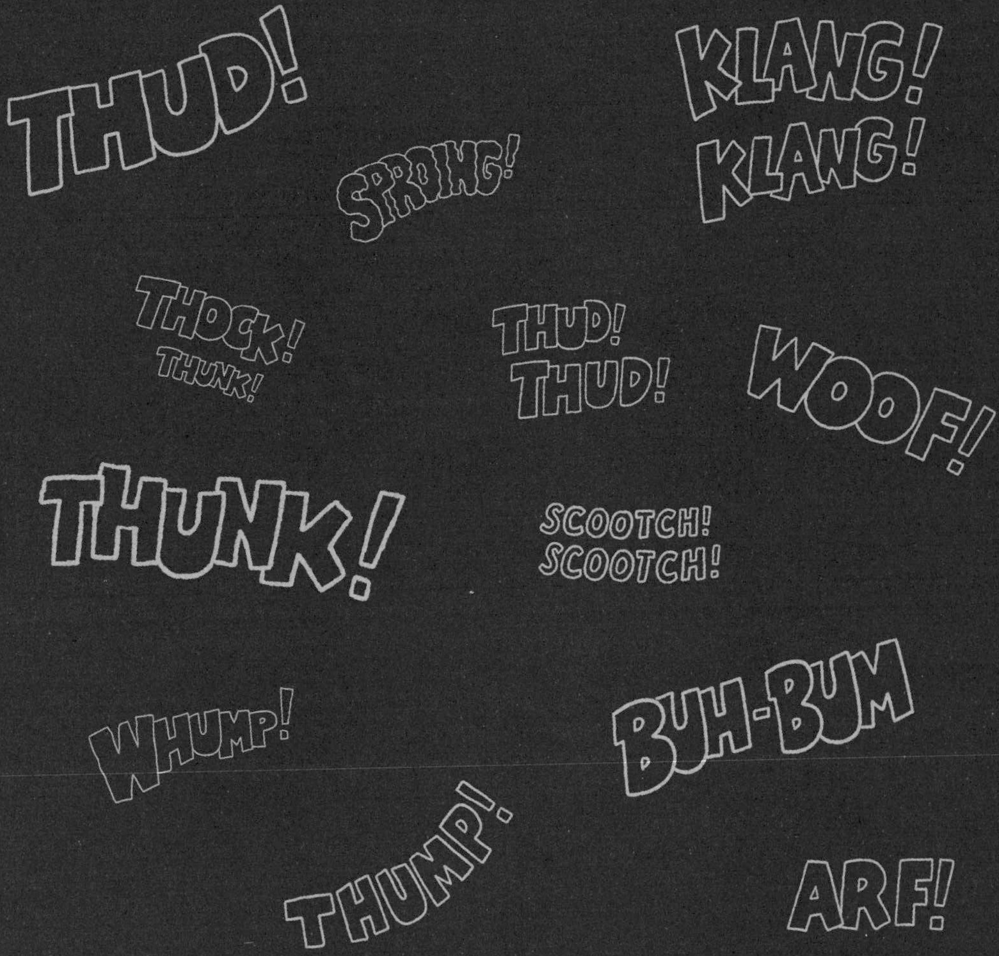
THUD!
SPROING!
KLANG! KLANG!
THOCK! THUNK!
THUD! THUD!
WOOF!
THUNK!
SCOOTCH! SCOOTCH!
WHUMP!
BUH-BUM
THUMP!
ARF!